EXPLORING
ANCIENT
CIVILIZATIONS

4

Drama – Great Wall of China

Marshall Cavendish

Marshall Cavendish
99 White Plains Road
Tarrytown, New York 10591-9001

www.marshallcavendish.com

Consultants: Daud Ali, School of Oriental and African
Studies, University of London; Michael Brett, School
of Oriental and African Studies, London; John
Chinnery, School of Oriental and African Studies,
London; Philip de Souza; Joann Fletcher; Anthony
Green; Peter Groff, Department of Philosophy,
Bucknell University; Mark Handley, History
Department, University College London; Anders
Karlsson, School of Oriental and African Studies,
London; Alan Leslie, Glasgow University Archaeology
Research Department; Michael E. Smith, Department
of Anthropology, University at Albany; Matthew
Spriggs, Head of School of Archaeology and
Anthropology, Australian National University

Contributing authors: Richard Balkwill, Richard
Burrows, Peter Chrisp, Richard Dargie, Steve Eddy,
Clive Gifford, Jen Green, Peter Hicks, Robert Hull,
Jonathan Ingoldby, Pat Levy, Steven Maddocks, John
Malam, Saviour Pirotta, Stewart Ross, Sean Sheehan,
Jane Shuter

WHITE-THOMSON PUBLISHING
Editors: Alex Woolf and Kelly Davis
Design: Derek Lee
Cartographer: Peter Bull Design
Picture Research: Glass Onion Pictures
Indexer: Fiona Barr

MARSHALL CAVENDISH
Editor: Thomas McCarthy
Editorial Director: Paul Bernabeo
Production Manager: Michael Esposito

Library of Congress Cataloging-in-Publication Data
Exploring ancient civilizations.
    p. cm.
Includes bibliographical references and indexes.
  ISBN 0-7614-7456-0 (set : alk. paper) -- ISBN 0-7614-7457-9 (v. 1 :
alk. paper) -- ISBN 0-7614-7458-7 (v. 2 : alk. paper) -- ISBN
0-7614-7459-5 (v. 3 : alk. paper) -- ISBN 0-7614-7460-9 (v. 4 : alk.
paper) -- ISBN 0-7614-7461-7 (v. 5 : alk. paper) -- ISBN 0-7614-7462-5
(v. 6 : alk. paper) -- ISBN 0-7614-7463-3 (v. 7 : alk. paper) -- ISBN
0-7614-7464-1 (v. 8 : alk. paper) -- ISBN 0-7614-7465-X (v. 9 : alk.
paper) -- ISBN 0-7614-7466-8 (v. 10 : alk. paper) -- ISBN 0-7614-7467-6
(v. 11 : alk. paper)
  1. Civilization, Ancient--Encyclopedias.
  CB311.E97 2004
  930'.03--dc21
                                    2003041224

ISBN 0-7614-7456-0 (set)
ISBN 0-7614-7460-9 (vol. 4)

Printed and bound in China

07 06 05 04 03 5 4 3 2 1

Contents

Drama

The word *drama* is generally used to mean a play, with actors performing a story for an audience. Drama in this sense was invented by the ancient Greeks around 530 BCE. Plays were later performed by the Romans (in imitation of the Greeks) and also in India. Although there is no evidence that dramatic performances involving actors and spectators developed in ancient times in Asia or Africa, the Egyptians used drama as part of their religious rituals.

The story of drama in the ancient world is mainly the story of Greek drama. In other parts of the ancient world, however, there were entertainers performing in other kinds of roles – as clowns, for instance. In Mayan paintings from about 100 CE, sacred clowns with fans and rattles seem to be taking the parts of gods. Perhaps in a similar way, the players – or performers – in the fierce Mesoamerican ball game were dramatizing, or acting out, a terrible sacred battle between the powers of good and evil, light and darkness.

In India drama developed, perhaps around 200 BCE, from the acting out of parts of religious poems called Vedic hymns. When passages of dialogue in the hymns were spoken by not one performer but two, one for each voice, the dramatized hymns inspired the writing of religious plays.

Ancient Greece

Greek drama developed in the sixth century BCE, also from religious hymns. In Athens, at celebrations in honor of Dionysus, the god of wine and pleasure, hymns were sung and danced to by a chorus. The hymns were called *tragedoi* (goat songs), from which comes the word *tragedy*. The goat was the animal sacred to Dionysus.

▶ *An ancient Greek theatre in Priene, Turkey, with a view toward the orchestra and the skene buildings behind it.*

The chorus danced and sang in unison. Then, some time in the sixth century BCE, a chorus leader, or trainer, experimented with having another performer stand opposite and answer the chorus. Now there were two voices – the chorus and an actor. In this way drama was invented. By the fifth century BCE some plays had a chorus and two or three actors.

Tragedy and Comedy

The Greeks wrote comic plays and tragedies. Tragedies concern serious events. Playwrights like Aeschylus, Sophocles, and Euripides wrote verse plays based on Greek myths and legends. Only thirty-two survive of hundreds that were written.

As the stories were already known, the drama was not in *what* would happen but in *how*. The Greeks believed that watching tragedies somehow "cleansed" the spectators' emotions and helped them understand good and evil. "We make men better," one playwright said.

▲ A Zapotec urn from Monte Albán, dating from around 600 BCE, in the shape of a player in a ball game.

AESCHYLUS FOUGHT AT THE VICTORIOUS BATTLE OF MARATHON IN 490 BCE. HERE A MESSENGER TELLS THE PERSIAN QUEEN MOTHER OF THE FIGHTING AT SALAMIS IN 479, WHEN THE PERSIANS WERE FINALLY DEFEATED:

At first the torrent of our Persian fleet
bore up; but when the crowd of ships started jamming
into each other in the narrows, no one could help anyone else.
Our ships rammed each other, got in each other's way
and broke each others' oars. But the Greek ships…
kept on surrounding us and striking into us, until our ships
keeled over, and you could not see the water
for blood and wreckage.… The Greeks
were hacking at our men in the water
with broken oars and bits of wreckage
the way fishermen kill tuna.

AESCHYLUS, *THE PERSIANS*

Comedies were meant to be funny, with plenty of singing, dancing, impolite jokes, and slapstick, and the jokes were aimed at situations and people in real life: war, corrupt juries, and famous politicians.

Greek plays were staged as part of religious festivals. Admission was free to those who could not afford to pay. Women probably attended, too. Drama was seen as an important part of every Athenian's education.

AESCHYLUS *525–456 BCE*

Aeschylus was a dramatist living in fifth-century-BCE Athens. He fought against the invading Persians at the Battle of Marathon in 490 and probably also at the final victory over the Persians at Salamis in 479. His play *The Persians* tells the story of the invasion from the Persian point of view.

Aeschylus took most of his stories from Greek myth. *The Oresteia*, his most famous trilogy – a group of three plays on one theme – begins when the Greek chief Agamemnon returns home after the war with Troy. He is murdered by his wife, Clytemnestra, helped by her lover Aegisthus, because Agamemnon had sacrificed their youngest daughter, Iphigenia, to help the ships sail for Troy.

Aeschylus changed the way in which drama was performed. He introduced a second speaking actor onto the stage and used visual stage effects and lavish costumes. He wrote about ninety plays, but only seven have survived. He was a popular dramatist and won first prize thirteen times in the drama competitions held at festivals in honor of the god Dionysus.

◀ *A fifth-century-BCE vase on which a Greek actor holds up a mask of the god Dionysus, who carried his panther skin with him.*

SEE ALSO
- Athens • Greece, Classical
- Greek Mythology • Hinduism
- Indus Valley • Maya

Dunhuang

Dunhuang was an important city in ancient China. From the second century BCE it was a busy trading center. The nearby caves at Mogao Ku also became a major center for Buddhist art. Dunhuang lies in northwest China, a region of rolling sand dunes and barren, empty deserts. The city was one of the few green oases in the area, where water was plentiful enough for farmers to grow crops. From a small settlement Dunhuang grew to major size under the Han emperors, who ruled China from 206 BCE to 220 CE.

After the Han dynasty was overthrown in 220 CE, China became divided into several smaller states. For nearly four centuries, until Sui emperors reunited the country in 589 CE, there was no centralized control. During this time, known as the Period of Disunity, Dunhuang became a semi-independent city.

The Great Wall

The town lay at the western terminus of the Great Wall of China, a defensive wall built in the third century BCE. From Dunhuang the Great Wall stretched right across China as far as the Yellow Sea. It was built to keep nomadic tribes from the north out of the Chinese empire. A large military force was stationed at the garrison at Dunhuang.

The Silk Road

The city owed its wealth to its position on the Silk Road, the ancient trade route that stretched from China west as far as the Mediterranean. Dunhuang was situated at the western end of the Silk Road's route through China. It was therefore the first town in China reached by merchants traveling from the west. Merchants, with their caravans of camels, trekked west along the route bearing Chinese silk and spices and returned with goods from Europe and the Middle East.

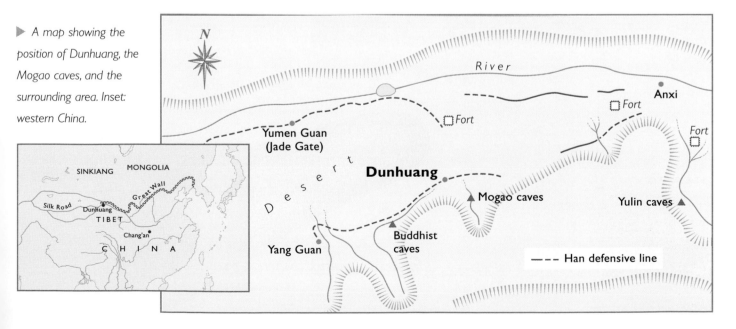

▶ A map showing the position of Dunhuang, the Mogao caves, and the surrounding area. Inset: western China.

The Spread of Buddhism

The Silk Road conveyed not only goods but also ideas and foreign influences. The Buddhist religion was founded in the sixth century BCE by an Indian prince named Siddhartha Gautama, who became known as Buddha. From the first century CE Buddhist monks traveled along the route to spread their faith. A string of towns in China along the Silk Road, including Dunhuang, became centers of Buddhist faith and art.

THE CAVES AT MOGZAO KU

▼ This fresco of Buddha teaching decorates one of the caves at Mogao Ku. It dates from between the fourth and sixth centuries CE.

In the 360s CE Buddhist monks began to excavate and decorate a group of caves at Mogao Ku, fifteen miles (24 km) east of Dunhuang. More and more of these caves were made into shrines over the next centuries. By around 1100 CE Mogao Ku held over a thousand shrines, richly decorated with murals and sculptures. Some have since been destroyed but about five hundred survive today.

The Mogao caves are mostly rectangular in shape, with beautiful murals on the walls and ceilings. Some have carved pillars that help to support the roof. The artists plastered the cave walls with straw and mud before applying pigments in a fresco technique. Most of the paintings show Buddha and his disciples. The colors, ranging from rich blues and greens to glowing reds and browns, were mainly made by crushing local minerals.

The centerpieces of each shrine are painted statues of Buddha. During the Period of Disunity, sculptors made these figures slim and graceful, according to Indian artistic traditions. After the late sixth century, when Chinese emperors reunified China, the figures are more solid, reflecting Chinese traditions in art.

SEE ALSO
- Buddha
- Buddhism
- China
- Chinese Philosophy
- Trade

Education

Learning took a variety of forms in early civilizations. Most young people learned about their place in the world by growing up in it and learning to do what their parents did. A boy might learn to fish or hunt by going out with his father and helping him. Similarly, a girl would learn tasks from her mother. The family was also where children learned the values of their society: what it thought was right and wrong, and what it believed in.

Early civilizations needed scribes, people who could read sacred writings, copy them down, and communicate them to others. Writing first appeared in Egypt around 3250 BCE. It seems that scribes never made up more than one percent of the population at that time. In Mesoamerica, where writing existed by 600 BCE, the carved hieroglyphs (inscriptions) at Oaxaca, not yet deciphered, could have been read only by trained scribes and priests.

▶ *This Mayan terra-cotta figure of a scribe writing was sculpted between 600 and 900 CE.*

Scribe schools

Scribes had to be trained. Mayan pots show illustrations of groups of scribes being taught to write and count. Scribes would practice writing on easily available or throwaway materials, such as clay in Mesopotamia, bits of broken rock or pottery in Greece and Egypt, and bark and leaves in Mexico and India.

Mesopotamian scribes went to schools called *edubba*. From about 3000 BCE excavated tablets record details of school life. One student describes being beaten nine times in one day. Math was important, as were law and medicine.

In ancient Egypt schools were for young men training to be scribes, either as priests or civil administrators. The main subjects were reading, handwriting, and arithmetic. There were punishments – beatings and copying out stories.

An ancient Egyptian schoolboy used this book of thin wooden slats in which to do his writing exercises.

Textbooks

In Egypt books of instruction were sometimes written by important officials for their children and colleagues. *The Instruction of Ptahhotep*, written by a high official in the twenty-third century BCE, has this advice: "Have conversation with uneducated people as well as the educated.... Wise thought and talk is as rare as the precious green stone, but you can find it amongst servant girls at their grindstones."

Values and Beliefs

Writing was not always necessary for one of the most important kinds of education in early civilizations – teaching people how to live. Children learned from their families the values they grew up with. Those values and beliefs, however, were often first proclaimed by great teachers, such as Jesus of Nazareth. The great Chinese teacher Confucius, a wandering wise man of the sixth century BCE, said that men and women should revere their parents and that rulers should rule for the benefit of their people.

Learning by Heart

After writing was invented but before there were many books or many readers, people often learned by memorizing. In India, from the end of childhood up until

AUSONIUS, A FOURTH-CENTURY-CE CHRISTIAN POLITICIAN AND POET, ASSUMES HIS GRANDCHILD WILL BE FRIGHTENED OF THE TEACHER:

Don't shudder at your teacher's appearance. He may scare you because he is old; and his harsh words and fierce expression might make you think he didn't like you at all. But if you can keep calm and don't get upset, he will not seem like a monster. And you don't need to be frightened even when the old man's face is full of fury and the schoolroom resounds with the noise of beating.

marriage, boys would live in the house of a guru, or teacher, learning subjects such as arithmetic, astrology, archery, and music. They also learned the two great stories, the *Ramayana* and the *Mahabharata*, and memorized endless verses of the Vedas – a collection of poems and hymns dating from around 1500 BCE. They learned orally, though some writing was done on bark and leaves. Some learning also took place with other students at an ashram. A boy's education could last a total of twelve years.

Spreading the Word

A sympathetic ruler might help spread these teachings. Ashoka, emperor of India from 268 to 232 BCE, became a follower of Buddha, a holy man born in the sixth century BCE. Buddha had taught people to despise worldly possessions and success. Ashoka had pillars of stone built all over his empire inscribed with some of Buddha's teachings. Ashoka outlawed the killing of animals for sport and taught respect for all living things. Many of his pillars stand to this day, still teaching those messages.

Greek Schools

The Indian ashram was not a school in the modern sense, an institution providing a formal education. Schools for the young did develop, however, in Greece and Rome. By law Greek citizens were expected to educate their male children. Girls, meanwhile, stayed at home, where their mothers taught them how to run a household. The city-states did not provide schools. Schoolteachers were paid directly by parents.

▼ *In this wall painting from Pompeii, a young woman with a waxed wooden writing tablet and stylus muses on what she wants to write.*

There were three kinds of schools in ancient Greece, each with a different kind of teacher. When they were about seven, boys went to the *grammatistes*, who taught reading, writing, and probably some arithmetic. Later, the *kitharistes*, the music teacher, taught them poetry, lyre and flute playing, and dancing. At about twelve, boys would go to the *paidotribes* to learn wrestling, running, and throwing the discus and javelin. To all these schools, richer boys would be accompanied by their *pedagogos*, a slave escort who stayed to watch over the boy and punish him if necessary.

Boys stayed at school until they were about fifteen. Then, if they wished, they might go to a gymnasium, a place where they could exercise and where they could also study more advanced subjects such as astronomy, geometry, and science.

SEE ALSO

• Children • Confucianism
• Greek Philosophy • Jesus of Nazareth
• Mahabharata • Maya • Writing

THE LAWS OF MANU

The sacred words of moral and religious teaching were sometimes kept for the few. Around the first century CE in India, many Hindu sayings, or sutras, were gathered together in a collection known as the Laws of Manu. The laws state that when the world was created, there were four classes of people. The duty of the top class, called Brahmins, was to study and teach the Vedas. The two next classes, the Kshatriyas (kings and warriors) and Vaisyas (farmers and merchants), could study the Vedas. The bottom group, however, the Sudras (serfs and slaves), were not allowed to read the Vedas and might even be punished for accidentally overhearing them by having molten lead poured into their ears.

▼ Boys at school in ancient Rome, as depicted in a sculpted stone relief from the second century CE.

Egypt

The ancient Egyptian civilization began about 5,000 years ago and lasted for over 3,000 years. The first people to live in Egypt, around 7000 BCE, were hunters and fishermen. These people settled along the banks of the River Nile and began to farm the land. At first there were two separate kingdoms – Upper and Lower Egypt. In about 3100 BCE the ruler of Upper Egypt, who was known as either Menes or Narmer, took over Lower Egypt and ruled them both as their king, or pharaoh.

▼ *Ancient Egypt during the period of the New Kingdom, which lasted from about 1550 to 1085 BCE.*

The River Nile

Egypt is a hot country with very little rain. People could live there only because the River Nile ran through it. Every year the river flooded from July to October. When the water went down, it left a layer of thick, black mud that was very good for growing crops in. So the ancient Egyptians lived in villages and towns along the banks of the river with farmland all around. They built their towns and villages high enough above the farmland to stay dry when the Nile flooded.

Houses

Although temples were built from stone, ordinary homes and even palaces were built from mud bricks. The homes were quite small, with flat roofs, small high windows, and wooden doors. The ancient Egyptians spent most of their time outside, cooking, eating, and even sleeping on the roof. Important people had bigger homes, often built around a courtyard with a garden.

Pharaohs

The kings of ancient Egypt, called pharaohs, ruled both the country and Egypt's religion. Egyptians believed the king was the son of the gods. They saw the pharaohs as their link to the gods, sometimes even as gods themselves.

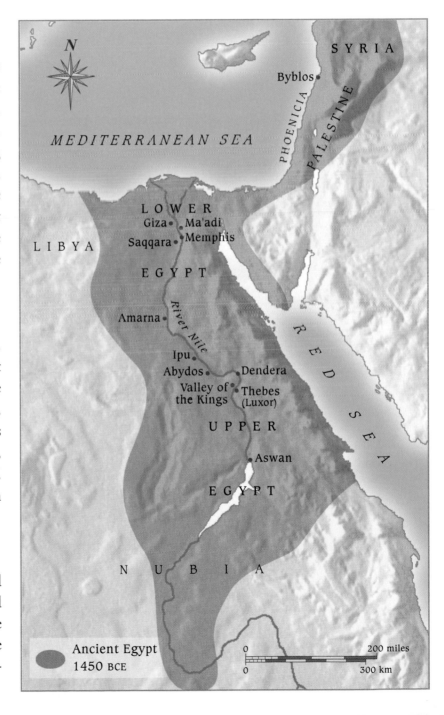

AKHENATEN *c. 1352–1336 BCE*

Akhenaten was the only pharaoh in Egypt's history to fundamentally change the country's religious practice, from the worship of many gods and goddesses to the worship of just one – the sun god, the most important god in Egypt. However, Akhenaten worshiped him as Aten rather than by the more familiar name, Ra. When Akhenaten died, his successors discarded his reforms, and the practice of worshiping many gods and goddesses resumed. The temples to Aten were pulled down, and Akhenaten's new capital city, Amarna, was abandoned. People were forbidden to talk about Akhenaten, and he was referred to simply as "the criminal."

▶ *This statuette of Akhenaten and his wife, Nefertiti, was made in Akhenaten's new capital city, Amarna. It is an example of the new, more realistic style of art that Akhenaten introduced, named by modern scholars the Amarna style after Akhenaten's city.*

The pharaohs ruled the country by dividing it into areas run by governors. The pharaoh and the governors had lots of officials working for them who kept records and made sure that things ran smoothly. When a pharaoh was strong, this system worked well. When a pharaoh was weak, the governors and chief officials sometimes took over the running of their regions, and thus, during these periods, Egypt was no longer ruled as one country. Historians call these times intermediate periods.

Gods and Goddesses

The Egyptians worshiped many gods and goddesses, each controlling a part of everyday life. It was important to please the gods. If Hapi, god of the Nile, was angry, he could stop the Nile from flooding, and people would starve. People prayed at outdoor shrines in towns or on the riverbank or at shrines in their homes. Temples were built as homes for the gods and goddesses. Ordinary people had access to the outer parts. Only the pharaoh and priests and priestesses were allowed to enter the inner areas of a temple.

Priests and priestesses worked in the temple every day. Here they looked after a statue of the god or goddess within which the deity's spirit was thought to live. Only the high priest of the temple went into the shrine to care for the god. Priestesses usually sang and danced in the temple to entertain the gods. Only high-ranking people could become high priests and priestesses.

ANCIENT EGYPT

c. 3100–2686 BCE

Early dynastic period.

c. 2686–2181 BCE

Old Kingdom.

c. 2181–2040 BCE

First intermediate period.

c. 2040–1795 BCE

Middle Kingdom.

c. 1795–1550 BCE

Second intermediate period.

c. 1550–1085 BCE

New Kingdom.

c. 1085–664 BCE

Third intermediate period.

664–332 BCE

Late period.

332–30 BCE

Greek (Ptolemaic) period.

30 BCE–395 CE

Roman period.

◀ *A painting from the Book of the Dead of the scribe Neferronpet, who helped the pharaoh Ramses II rule Thebes during the last years of his reign. Neferronpet was wealthy as well as important. The scribe kneels as he prays to Anubis, the jackal god of embalming and guardian of cemeteries.*

Ordinary people could work as lower members of the priesthood and prepare the sacred offerings or tend the sacred cattle.

Death and the Afterlife

The ancient Egyptians believed in a life after death. Everyone who died was taken to the underworld, the world of the dead. Here the gods judged each man and woman. A person who had led a good life went to the Field of Reeds to live forever. Otherwise, a creature called Ammut ate the person's heart, and the person would thus be completely destroyed.

The ancient Egyptians also believed it was important to preserve the body of the dead person. At first the dead were buried in the hot desert sands, which soaked up the fluids and preserved the bodies naturally. Later, the ancient Egyptians began to bury important people in wooden coffins in tombs, along with many of their possessions for use in the afterlife. The bodies rotted, however, because the sand no longer preserved them; so the Egyptians developed a way of preserving bodies by embalming them. At first only pharaohs and very important people were embalmed. As time passed, more and more people were embalmed.

Tombs of the Pharaohs

The most famous burial site of pharaohs is the Valley of the Kings, where tombs were cut deep into the rock to make them harder to find. Pharaohs were buried here all through the New Kingdom period (1550 to 1069 BCE). Other members of royal families were buried in the nearby Valley of the Queens. The tombs were built and decorated by workmen who lived near the valleys and who were forbidden to tell anyone where the tombs were.

The tomb workers of the Valley of the Kings lived in their own village close to the desert. All their food and water was brought up on donkeys. When supplies did not arrive on time, they sometimes stopped working and went on strike.

▼ *These rooms in the tomb of Queen Nefertari in the Valley of the Queens were restored in the 1990s, using original painting techniques.*

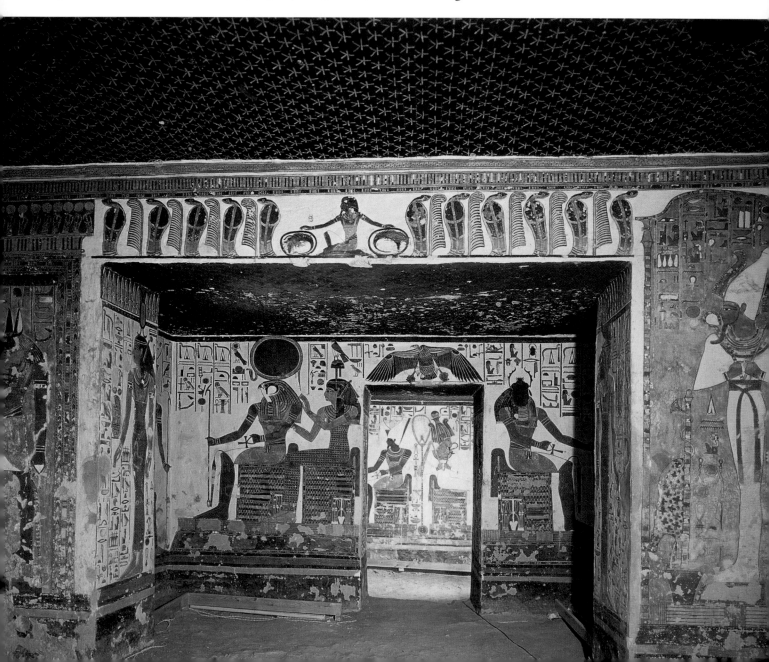

MUMMIES

Mummies *is the modern name given to the embalmed bodies of ancient Egyptians and other peoples. The ancient Egyptians mummified their dead because they believed that it was important to preserve a person's body so that he or she could live forever. They believed a person had six parts, which were separated when a person died and had to reunite in the afterlife. The six parts were a body, a name, a shadow, a* ka *(a double of the body that lived forever, often regarded as the soul), a* ba, *or personality, and an* akh, *a transfigured spirit formed when the* ka *and* ba *reunited.*

The ancient Egyptians worked out a way to preserve bodies by drying them out and wrapping them in strips of linen. The people who made mummies were called embalmers. The process of embalming took a long time. The embalmers removed all the soft internal organs, leaving just the heart behind for the gods to judge. They covered the body in a kind of salt called natron for forty days to soak up the fluids. Then they washed the body and coated it in resin to protect it from moisture. Finally they wrapped it in linen strips, which could also be soaked with resin. As much as 550 square yards (500 m²) of linen were used.

How a body was embalmed depended on how much the relatives of the dead person could pay. Only pharaohs and high-ranking officials could afford the most expensive treatment. As embalmers wrapped the body, they placed between the layers many amulets — magical charms to protect the body. Archeologists have found some cheaper mummies wrapped in recycled clothing and even boat sails.

▼ *This mummy case, found in Thebes (Luxor) and dating to around 1000 BCE, belonged to a priest whose name is not known.*

Pyramids

Pyramids were monumental tombs for pharaohs. They were not built during the whole ancient Egyptian period, only from about 2650 to 1800 BCE. The actual tomb was either underground or in the center of the pyramid – the pyramid itself was a display of the power of the pharaoh. The earliest pyramids were built in steps. They were built entirely from stone. The most famous pyramids are the three great pyramids at Giza. The biggest, the pyramid of the pharaoh Khufu, took over twenty years to build. The base is a square, 755 feet (230 m) on each side, and the height is 479 feet (146 m). It was built from over 2.3 million limestone blocks, which were covered in the finest white limestone so that it would shine in the sunlight.

Farming and Food

Every year the River Nile flooded from July to October. When the water went down, it left a layer of thick, rich mud, fertile enough for farmers to grow several different crops. They plowed the fields as the river fell and sowed wheat or barley, which they harvested in March. Then they grew vegetables, such as beans, onions, and cabbage, before the river rose again. In most years farmers grew enough to feed everyone, with some left over to store for bad harvest years and for trade.

In some years the Nile did not flood much; in other years not at all. The Egyptians built Nilometers: steps down into the river with marks for measuring the water level each year. When officials saw the river was rising too slowly, they had to plan for a year with bad crops. If there were several bad years, the store of food would run out, and people starved.

Trade

The ancient Egyptians grew or made almost everything they needed, and they traded with each other at local markets. They did not use money; instead, they swapped goods. For example, a sandalmaker might swap sandals for food or cloth or for more leather to make sandals with. Most ordinary people lived fairly simply and did not need a lot of possessions.

The ancient Egyptians also traded with nearby countries. They traded grain, rope, papyrus paper, perfumes, and linen for goods such as gold, silver, precious stones, and spices. All these traded goods were

▼ *This is the earliest known pyramid, built at Saqqara for the pharaoh Djoser, who died in about 2648 BCE. It was designed by Imhotep, Djoser's chief adviser, who was later worshiped as the god of medicine.*

things that ordinary Egyptians could not afford. Historians believe that officials of the pharaoh or of the most important people in the country did most of the trading. Trading journeys were often expensive and difficult because Egypt was largely cut off from the rest of the world by deserts or the sea.

Clothes

Egypt was a hot country, so people did not need to wear a lot of clothing. Workers wore clothes that were simple and let them move and work easily. Men wore a short kilt, women a long tunic. More important people wore longer, more complicated clothes. Most clothes were made from linen cloth, made from the flax plant. Both men and women wore jewelry and makeup. Many people shaved their head or cut their hair very short to keep cool, and some wore wigs on special occasions.

Language and Writing

The ancient Egyptians had two kinds of writing, and scholars can decipher both of them. Hieroglyphs, a kind of picture writing where the pictures show both sounds and whole words, were difficult to learn and were mostly used on things that were made to last, such as the walls of temples or tombs. For everyday letters and lists the ancient Egyptians used hieratic, which was a quicker method of writing. However, most Egyptians did not write at all. Writing was a special skill practiced only by specially trained scribes.

A MESSAGE FROM TOMB WORKERS IN THE VALLEY OF THE KINGS SENT TO THE PHARAOH:

We are hungry and thirsty. We have no clothes, no oils, no fish, and no vegetables. We write this to the pharaoh, so that he will give us the means to live.

▲ *This tomb model came from the tomb of Mesehti, a governor of ancient Egypt. It shows foot soldiers on the march. In real life the governor would have had control of an army, so he needed one in the afterlife, too.*

War

Egypt was largely cut off from other lands by the desert and the sea and thus was well protected. Even so, there were times when other countries attacked Egypt and times when Egypt sent armies to other countries to conquer more land. The ancient Egyptians fought mostly on land, not at sea or on the river. Their soldiers fought with spears, daggers, slings, and bows and arrows.

After horses were brought to Egypt in about 1600 BCE, some soldiers fought from war chariots. The chariots were very light, with big wheels and a small platform that could hold just two people. One person drove while the other fired arrows or spears.

THE ANCIENT EGYPTIANS WROTE DOWN ALL KINDS OF THINGS, INCLUDING LISTS OF STORES, LAUNDRY LISTS, LETTERS, SPELLS, PRAYERS, AND SACRED WRITING IN TOMBS. THEY ALSO WROTE POEMS. HERE IS PART OF ONE:

She looks like the morning star
At the start of a happy year.
Shining bright, fair of skin,
Lovely the look of her eyes,
Sweet the speech of her lips,
She says not a word too much.

SEE ALSO

- Amenhotep III • Amun • Book of the Dead
- Cleopatra • Egyptian Mythology • Giza
- Hatshepsut • Kushan Empire • Nefertiti
- Ramses II • Thebes • Tutankhamen
- Valley of the Kings

Egyptian Mythology

The ancient Egyptians believed in many different gods and goddesses, all of which could affect their lives. The gods could stop the sun from shining or the River Nile from flooding, so they had to be kept happy to ensure life ran smoothly. The myths of ancient Egypt are stories about the gods that were told to people from the time they were children and were passed on from generation to generation. The myths explained who the gods were and why nature worked as it did. They were told as stories and also sung as hymns to the gods.

The ancient Egyptians believed that the gods controlled nature and could cause all kinds of natural disasters. It was important that everyone understood how important the gods were and how to keep them happy through prayers, dancing, and constant attention.

Temples were homes for the gods where the priests cared for statues of the gods, dressing them, feeding them, and making offerings to them daily, as if they were the gods themselves. Ordinary people were not allowed into the temples to worship. They prayed at shrines on the outside of temple walls or in their homes. While priests worshiped important gods, such as Amun, ordinary people also prayed to the gods who they believed controlled ordinary life, such as Bes, a household god who protected women and children and drove away evil spirits.

The gods also controlled Egypt in another way, by helping to choose the pharaoh. If they chose a strong pharaoh, Egypt would prosper. If the chosen pharaoh was weak, Egypt might become divided or be poorly ruled, and as a result, the people would be in danger of starving.

◀ The River Nile and the modern village of Karnak. The modern houses are small, built, as ancient Egyptian homes were, from mud bricks. At the front of the picture are the stone outlines of two temples: the bigger one is the Temple of Amun, the smaller is the Temple of Mut. Made from stone, temples were built to last.

Pharaohs were seen as the sons of the gods and the link between the people and the gods. They were more than human but not actual gods. Many pharaohs, especially strong ones, were treated increasingly like gods. After they died, they were worshiped in specially built mortuary temples.

The First Gods

During the early period of Egypt's history, until about 3100 BCE, people worshiped aspects of nature, such as mountains, the River Nile, and animals. The objects worshiped developed into gods and goddesses that were more like people, with families and ordinary emotions. They were given names, and each god and goddess was responsible for a different part of life.

Gods and goddesses were worshiped in different places along the River Nile. For example, in the Delta area (at the mouth of the Nile) and in other places along the river that were troubled by crocodiles, people worshiped Sobek, the crocodile god.

Although these gods and goddesses resembled humans, they also had animal sides to them. Paintings and statues of the gods showed them with the head of an animal on a human body. Thoth, the god of wisdom and learning, for example, was shown with an ibis head. He was first worshiped in the Delta region and then in Middle Egypt before being worshiped all through Egypt. As god of the scribes, he was often shown recording things in paintings and sculptures.

▼ *This wooden mummy case of Nespawershepi, chief priest at the Temple of Amun, shows one of the many myths about how the sun rises and sets. The sun god, Ra, sails in his golden boat across the sky each morning and kills the serpent of darkness that represents the night.*

The Story of Sunrise

In the time before Egypt was one country, people living in different places developed their own myths about why things happened. When Egypt was united, these different stories continued to be told. For example, there are several different myths about how the sun rises and sets.

According to one myth, the sky goddess, Nut, stretches over the earth and swallows the sun each night. The sun then travels through her body before being reborn each morning.

Although the sun is most often shown in paintings as the god Ra with a human body and falcon's head, the sun could also be shown as Khepri, god of the rising sun, represented as a scarab beetle who pushes the sun through the sky in the same way the beetle pushes dung balls along. The sunrise was seen as the falcon god Horus, whose name means "the far one." The sunset was the elderly god Atum.

The myths probably grew up in early times in different parts of Egypt. The ancient Egyptians did not believe that there was one correct version of the myth. They were all possible.

Amun

Pharaohs came from different parts of Egypt, and the local gods from a pharaoh's home region would become more powerful during his reign. The most important of all the gods, for most of Egypt's history, was Amun, who began as the local god of the area around Thebes. As Amun Ra he was combined with Ra, the sun god, to become the king of the gods.

▶ *This golden ornament shows the household god Bes. He was a kindly god, but he is always shown as fierce-looking because it was his job to scare away evil spirits.*

THE FOLLOWING PASSAGE COMES FROM A HYMN TO HAPI, GOD OF THE NILE:

Lord of the fish, he sends the wild birds south as he rises
He is father to the barley and the wheat
If he is slow to rise, the people hold their breath
They grow fierce as the food runs short.
When he rises well, the people and the land rejoice.

▶ *This painting from the Book of the Dead shows a dead nobleman praying to the hippopotamus goddess Taweret. The cow-shaped figure to the left is the goddess Hathor, shown here emerging from the sand of the cemetery in her role as goddess of the West and protector of the dead.*

Because Amun means "the hidden one," whom none can know, there are relatively few stories about Amun himself. He often appears in myths toward the end to put things right. The ancient Egyptians disliked talking about powerful people directly. This fact may explain why Amun does not have many of his own myths.

Creation Myths

One of the Egyptian myths of creation had the sun god, Ra, born out of the waters of chaos to bring order and light. He made the twin gods Shu and Tefnut, who produced the earth god Geb and the sky goddess Nut, who in turn had four children: Osiris, Isis, Seth, and Nephthys.

Recording Myths

The myth of Osiris and his family was told all over Egypt. This myth was important to the ancient Egyptians because it was connected to their ideas about rulers and about the afterlife. Myths were also recorded in temples. Because of these records, scholars know about the goddess Hathor, for example, who is shown as a cow, as a woman with a cow's ears, or as a woman with a headdress made up of cow's horns and a sun disk. Hathor was the goddess of love, beauty, and pleasure, who protected women in childbirth. She was connected with foreign places and was the goddess of the desert. Hathor was the powerful daughter of Ra and the wife of Horus.

THE MYTH OF OSIRIS

Osiris ruled Egypt and was married to his sister Isis. His brother Seth was very jealous of him and decided to kill Osiris and take over Egypt. Seth held a feast for Osiris and many other people, and at the end of the feast, he said he would give a beautiful cedarwood chest to the person who fitted into it best. Osiris was the last to climb in. As soon as he was in, Seth slammed on the lid and nailed it shut and threw it into the Nile.

In one version of the story, the chest floated down the Nile into the Mediterranean and washed up at Byblos, in modern-day Lebanon. A tree grew up all around it, so big that the king of Byblos used it as a pillar in his palace. Isis searched for Osiris and, by her powerful magic, found him. The king of Byblos gave her the pillar. She took Osiris's body out and hid it in the reeds of the marshy delta, where the Nile joins the Mediterranean.

Seth, hunting in the delta, found Osiris's body. He was furious and hacked it to pieces and scattered the parts all through Egypt. Isis had to find all the parts. With the assistance of Anubis and Thoth, Isis embalmed Osiris and made him whole. Once Isis had revived Osiris with her magic, they had a son, Horus, who went on to defeat Seth and avenge his father. Osiris became ruler of the underworld.

▼ This painting from the tomb of Queen Nefertari shows Osiris as ruler of the underworld.

Hymns and Spells

Ancient Egyptian myths were woven into hymns to the gods and goddesses and also into magic spells. Hymns and magic spells were said to the gods to ask for help. Doctors chanted spells while they gave medicine to a patient, to ask the god to make the medicine work.

SEE ALSO

- Amenhotep III
- Amun
- Book of the Dead
- Egypt • Thebes

Elamites

The Elamites lived in the country of Elam, in what is now southwest Iran. The civilization's early history and culture is closely linked with that of Sumer in Mesopotamia, its close neighbor to the south.

The origins of Elam are linked with the Sumerian civilization that developed in the fertile plains of the Euphrates and Tigris Rivers; the first Elamite kings emerged around 2700 BCE. The history of the Elamites stretches over a long period, involving successes and failures against the rival powers of Assyria and Babylon, before coming to an end in 639 BCE.

In that year, Susa, an Elamite royal city at the foot of the Zagros Mountains, was looted and destroyed by Ashurbanipal of Assyria. He recorded the event as an act of revenge for earlier defeats of the Mesopotamians: "I destroyed the land of the Elamites and on their lands I sowed salt," he said.

▼ A map of Elamite territory during the mid-twelfth century BCE.

Old Elam

The early kings of Elam were in conflict with the Mesopotamian city of Ur. Periods of warfare probably interrupted longer periods of peace, but sometime around 2080 BCE the land of Elam was conquered by King Shulgi of Ur. There followed a period of submission to Ur, but Mesopotamian accounts record a rebellion by the Elamites that resulted in a new Elamite dynasty known as the Eparti.

In time there were new conflicts with the emerging power of Babylon, and Elam was conquered in 1764 BCE by the Babylonian king Hammurabi. As with Ur, a period of submission was followed by an uprising. Around 1712 BCE the son of

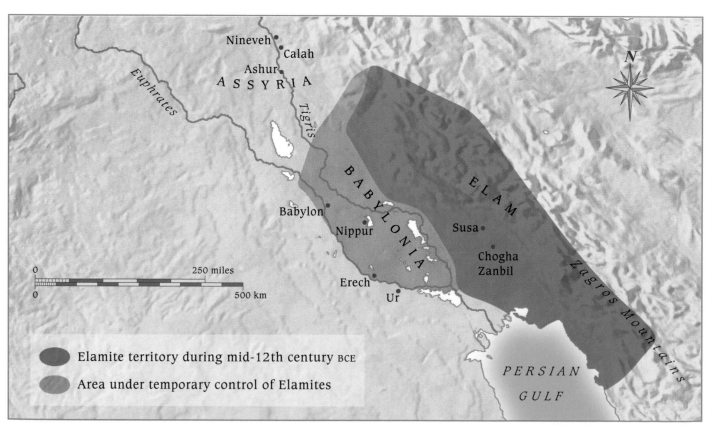

Elamite territory during mid-12th century BCE

Area under temporary control of Elamites

ELAMITES

2700 BCE

First kings of Old Elam.

2080 BCE

Elam conquered by Ur.

1764 BCE

Elam defeated by Hammurabi of Babylon.

c. 1712 BCE

Elamite victory over Babylon.

1500 BCE

End of Old Elam.

c. 1285–1266 BCE

Reign of Khumbannumena in Middle Elamite period.

639 BCE

Susa is pulled down by the Assyrians.

Hammurabi was attacked and defeated by Kutir-Nahhunte I of Elam. Nothing is known about the decline of the Eparti dynasty, but by the end of the sixteenth century BCE, the history of Old Elam came to an end, and there followed two centuries of obscurity.

Middle and Late Elam

The land of Elam covered highlands to the north and northeast as well as lowlands that formed part of the Mesopotamian plain.

KING KHUMBANNUMENA
c. 1285–1266 BCE

The Anshanite dynasty that emerged in the fourteenth century BCE marked the beginning of the middle period of Elamite history. It was a period that saw the reemergence of Elam as a political force, one that was able to exert control over its territory through strong leadership and military force. Evidence of success is to be found in the title that was claimed by King Khumbannumena, Expander of the Empire. His son, Untash-Gal, continued the expansion and founded the city named after him, Dur Untash (on the site of present-day Chogha Zanbil). One of his successors, Kidin-Khutran, was able successfully to confront the growing power of Assyria for a time but was eventually unable to fight off Assyrian intrusions into the Elamite lowlands in Mesopotamia. The Anshanite dynasty declined and passed out of history as a consequence.

◀ A headless bronze statue of Queen Napirasu, who became the daughter-in-law of King Khumbannumena after her marriage to Untash-Gal.

The highlands made a vital contribution to Elamite civilization because they provided the wood, stone, and metals that were lacking in the fertile lowland plains that supported agriculture.

The new dynasty of Elamite kings, called the Anshanite, that emerged toward the end of the fourteenth century BCE, are thought to have come from the highlands. The Anshanite kings paved the way for a prosperous new period when Elam established itself as a military power in the region. Beginning in the late thirteenth century, Elam extended its territory southward into central Mesopotamia. Babylon itself was sacked, but success was short-lived and Middle Elam fell to Babylonian forces early in the eleventh century BCE.

Between the eleventh century and 742 BCE, when a new king of Elam is recorded, Elam suffered a decline in power from which the Elamites never recovered. Power struggles between Elamite rulers weakened the state, and the growing power of Assyria threatened its future. The independent Elamite state came to an end in 639 BCE, when the Assyrian king Ashurbanipal sent his army to destroy Susa and deport its leading citizens. The new Susa that was later built over the ruins became an important city in the Persian Empire.

Elamite Culture

The Elamite language has been partly deciphered, but no religious texts have been found, nor works of literature that would shed light on Elamite beliefs and customs. It is known that a bull god, named Inshushinak, was worshiped and a temple at Chogha Zanbil was dedicated to this god. There was also a tradition of stargazing and star worship; this aspect of their culture may have influenced Mesopotamia.

Although Elam and Mesopotamia were periodically at war, there were periods of peaceful trade when ideas as well as goods were exchanged. Elamite art that has been found, in the form of statues and cylinder seals, resembles Mesopotamian art, but it is also distinctive in its use of glazed bricks and metalwork. Archaeologists have found evidence of extensive Elamite trade, including a type of bowl that has also been found in the Indus valley.

▶ *Riches, including rings and a whetstone, dating from the Middle Elamite period, around 1150 BCE.*

▲ The grand remains of
the Elamite ziggurat at
Chogha Zanbil, a palace
and temple complex near
Susa in present-day Iran.

CHOGHA ZANBIL

The most impressive example of Elamite architecture still standing is the complex of palaces and temples at Chogha Zanbil in what is now southwest Iran. Built around 1250 BCE by the Anzanite king Untash-Gal, the buildings stand upon an imposing ziggurat. The ziggurat's base, at ground level, forms a square with sides 344 feet (105 m) in length, and although its highest point is now 80 feet (24 m) above the ground, it was originally at least twice this height. The ziggurat is built of baked bricks, each one weighing forty pounds (18 kg), and gates at ground level led to various staircases that accessed the higher levels.

The main temple adorned the summit, a home for Inshushinak, who nightly ascended to the heavens, according to Elamite beliefs. Terra-cotta bulls stood guard on either side of the gates, and a wall surrounding the complex was adorned with sculptures. The Chogha Zanbil site was discovered only by accident in 1935, by an oil company surveying the land from an airplane.

SEE ALSO
• Ashurbanipal
• Babylonians
• Mesopotamia
• Shulgi • Sumer
• Ur

Ephesus

Ephesus, in present-day western Turkey, was one of the richest seaports in the ancient world. Founded by Greeks around 1100 BCE, the city was ruled in turn by the Lydians, the Persians, the Macedonians, and the Romans. However, they all allowed the Ephesians to get on with the business of trading and growing rich.

Ephesus prospered because many trade routes met there. Assyrian and Persian roads led from Ephesus to Babylonia. It was also the natural place for Greek and Roman merchant ships to land in search of Asian goods and customers. The city was surrounded by rich farming land; grain from the fertile Meander valley, near Ephesus, was sent from Asia Minor to feed Athens and Rome.

The Temple of Artemis

Artemis was an Asian fertility goddess. The Greeks adopted her as their goddess of wild animals and of hunting. The Romans worshiped her as Diana. The original temple of Artemis at Ephesus was built by the first Asian inhabitants. This building was replaced around 550 BCE by a grander temple funded by Croesus, the wealthy king of Lydia. A column from the temple, preserved in the British Museum, carries the inscription "the gift of Croesus."

Thousands of pilgrims made their way to the temple each year. Some came to worship at the huge statue of the goddess there. Others used the temple as a place of sanctuary from enemies. Merchants used the temple as a kind of bank, knowing they could leave their valuables in the safekeeping of the priestesses. Although it was damaged in several wars, the temple was one of the Seven Wonders of the World for over eight hundred years. It was destroyed in 262 CE, when the Ostrogoths captured and sacked the city.

▼ A city plan of ancient Ephesus. Inset: the location of Ephesus in the Greek world.

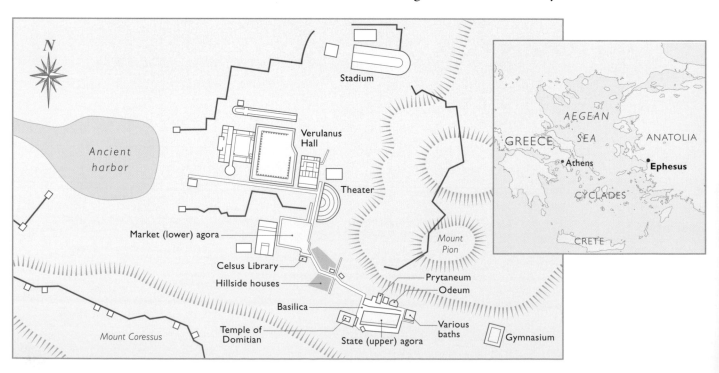

270 Ephesus

City Government

The leading citizens of Ephesus sat on the boule, or city council, and discussed how the city should be run. The Ephesians apparently enjoyed arguing. The philospher Heraclitus, who believed that everything in the world was constantly changing, came from a rich Ephesian family. Many Jewish traders in the city also enjoyed religious debates. Perhaps it was because of this openness to ideas that Ephesus was an early center of the new, controversial Christian religion.

Decline

Ephesus became part of the Roman Empire in 133 BCE. It remained very wealthy even after the fall of Rome in the fifth century CE. However, the city was badly damaged by a severe earthquake in 614 CE, and soon afterward it was repeatedly attacked by the Sasanians from Persia. As a result most of the merchants moved away to safer cities, such as Constantinople and Smyrna, and Ephesus slowly became a deserted city.

LYSIMACHUS *c. 360–281 BCE*

Lysimachus, a friend of Alexander the Great, ruled a small kingdom in Asia Minor and became overlord of Ephesus around 301 BCE. Lysimachus saw that Ephesus had grown up haphazardly. Traders had built their shops in the narrow streets around the Temple of Artemis to sell things to the pilgrims who came there. In 287 BCE Lysimachus founded a new, spacious city a mile (1.6 km) away, at the mouth of the River Cayster, and he built a fortified harbor where merchant ships could berth and store their goods. The harbor made Ephesus very rich until the Cayster silted up around 500 CE. The site of Lysimachus's city and harbor is now over six miles (9.6 km) inland.

SEE ALSO

- Alexander the Great • Christianity • Goths
- Greece, Classical • Greek Mythology • Paul of Tarsus
- Roads • Roman Mythology • Sasanians

Epidaurus

At Epidaurus, in the eastern Peloponnese, there is still much to see from ancient times. Its theater is probably the most famous and well-preserved site in the whole of the Greek world. The sanctuary at Epidaurus specialized in healing the sick and became very popular in the fourth century BCE.

▼ The lower section of the well-preserved theater at Epidaurus retains its fourth-century-BCE plan. This first phase of construction contained 34 rows of seats holding 6,200 spectators. A higher section of 21 rows, added later, took the theater's capacity to around 14,000.

The most sacred religious sites in ancient Greece were the *temenos* (sanctuaries, or sacred precincts). Excavation has shown that these sites, often containing temples, treasuries, statues, theaters, guest houses, baths, gymnasia, and stadia (running tracks), were highly complicated.

Epidaurus was associated with health because Asclepius, the Greek hero and god of healing, lived and worshiped there. Visitors went through cleansing and washing ceremonies conducted by the temple doctors and then slept in a special temple called an *abaton*. In the night a god would appear to them in a dream and suggest the correct treatment, which might involve therapies in the gymnasium or bath or even the use of snake bites.

The Theater

The theater at Epidaurus (from the Greek *theatron*, meaning "seeing place") was built during the fourth and third centuries BCE. It is carved out of the side of Mount Konyortos and contains fifty-five rows of seats accommodating thirteen to fourteen thousand spectators. Important guests sat in the more comfortable front-row seats, which had back rests. At the front was the orchestra – the place where the chorus danced and sang – which was a huge twenty-five yards (23 m) in diameter. The actors stood on a raised stage called a *proskenion*, twenty-six yards (24 m) long by eight feet (2.5 m) wide, with two extensions projecting at the sides. Behind it was the actors' changing room, or *skene*, from which come the words *scene* and *scenery*.

The Games

Every four years came the Asclepieia games, consisting of musical and sporting competitions dedicated to Asclepius. The

ASCLEPIUS

Asclepius was believed to be the son of Apollo and Coronis. It was said he was suckled by a goat after his mother was killed and then brought up by the centaur Chiron, who taught him the arts of healing. He was an earth god, and his symbol is a snake. His statue at Epidaurus showed him with a staff and sacred snake, the same way he appeared on the coins minted at the sanctuary. It is believed that Asclepius's sacred snakes were kept on the lower floor of the *tholos* (round building). Asclepius's powers were thought so great that after the plague struck Rome in 293 BCE, the Romans set up a temple and sanctuary to Asclepius based on the ones at Epidaurus.

stadium, like the theater, was impressive. Built between two hills, it was 235 yards long and 27 yards wide (215 by 25 m); rows of stone seats were built on three sides. However, the Asclepieia never really challenged the popularity of the Olympic or Pythian Games.

SEE ALSO

- Delphi • Drama • Games
- Greece, Classical • Greek Mythology

Erech

Erech, also known as Uruk, was one of the great Mesopotamian cities of Sumer. It was situated on the present-day site of Warka, in southeast Iraq. A wall of bricks surrounded the city of Erech, while outside lay the farms and smaller communities under its control. Archaeological work, which started on the site in 1849, has shown the walls to have been about six miles (10 km) in circumference. According to Mesopotamian tradition, the walls were built by the legendary hero Gilgamesh.

The earliest settlement at Erech seems to belong to around 4000 BCE. Urban life continued at Erech until the early third century CE, although the site is most important for what it reveals about the Sumerian culture of the late fourth and third millennia BCE.

History and Religion

During the early period of Erech's history, in the fourth millennium BCE, the city was both a political and an economic power in the region. During this time its influence reached as far as present-day Syria, Turkey, and Iran. It was also during this time, toward the end of the fourth millennium, that the world's earliest system of writing, known as proto-cuneiform, developed in Erech.

As with other powerful Sumerian cities, a kingship developed in Erech and with it a growing rivalry with neighboring kings and their territories. This period of rivalry and conflict lasted until around 2800 BCE. Then there emerged a union of the most powerful Sumerian cities, including Erech, under the influence of the king of Kish. This period did not last for very long, and

▼ A plan of ancient Erech, one of the world's earliest cities, showing the phases of its construction. Inset: the position of Erech in western Asia.

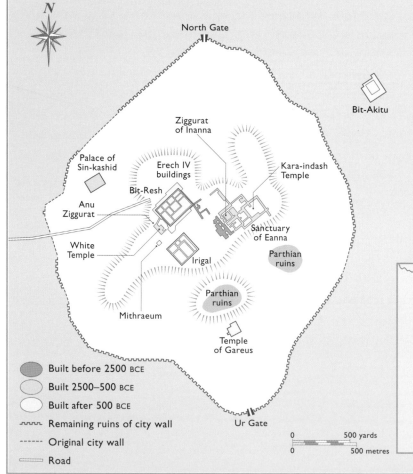

for more than two hundred years, Erech competed with Ur, Kish, and the city of Lagash for domination of Sumer. Interstate wars weakened Sumer, and Erech was eventually conquered by the Akkadians.

Erech was typical of the advanced cities of the Sumerian civilization. A pictograph from Erech showing a sleigh with wheels attached and dating from about 3500 BCE is part of the earliest evidence for the discovery of the wheel. Other archaeological finds indicate that the city boasted a high level of metalwork, particularly using gold and silver.

A religious festival at Erech celebrated the marriage of the goddess Inanna to Dumuzi-Amaushumgalana. Inanna – one of whose names was the Lady of the Date Clusters and who was called Ishtar by the Akkadians – was a fertility figure. The commemorating of her marriage was a symbolic celebration of the successful harvesting of crops.

▲ This relief carving from Erech, dated 3200–2900 BCE, shows the goddess Inanna, whom the Babylonians called Ishtar.

ENMEKER, THE HERO KING

Enmeker is a legendary king of Erech, said to have reigned sometime around 2000 BCE. According to Sumerian epics, Enmeker was the brother of the goddess Inanna and the child of the sun god, Utu. Three surviving epics relate stories of a conflict between Enmeker and the ruler of another city, Aratta, supposedly in the highlands of present-day Iran. In one tale, a priest arrives in Erech with a plan to defeat Enmeker but is outsmarted by a clever old woman called Sagburro.

Another epic relates the adventures of a faithful assistant to Enmeker, called Lugalbanda. He travels to Aratta to find Inanna, who can aid her brother in securing victory over the ruler of Aratta. Interestingly, one account refers to a promised exchange of grain to meet Enmeker's need of stone and metals from Aratta. The development of civilization depended on people from areas of fertile plains securing supplies of stone, wood, and metals from neighboring uplands. The importance of such trade is reflected in this legend about Enmeker.

SEE ALSO
• Akkadians • Cities • Gilgamesh Epic • Ishtar • Mesopotamia • Sumer • Ur

Eridu

Eridu is recorded in Sumerian written tradition as the earliest shrine and city in Sumer. The city dates from 5000 BCE or earlier and was occupied until about 400 BCE, when it fell into disuse and became covered with windswept sand. Eridu remained an undisturbed mound for over two thousand years until it was rediscovered in 1853. Systematic excavations took place between 1946 and 1949.

The city of Eridu arose in a unique location in Mesopotamia, between the desert to the south, marshlands to the east, and the River Euphrates to the north. The shrine at Eridu was revered as the home of Ea, god of the Abzu, an underground freshwater ocean, and of wisdom and magic. The Mesopotamians regarded Eridu as the birthplace of human life and the place where land first rose from the water. It was created as a city of dwelling places, according to Mesopotamian tradition, by a god pouring mud over a reed frame. Examples of mud huts built from reed frames are still in use by the marsh dwellers of southern Iraq.

Temples and Palaces

At the deepest layer of excavation at the site of Eridu, archaeologists unearthed a small shrine dated to around 5500 BCE. For the next fifteen hundred years, until around 4000 BCE, a succession of new and increasingly larger temples was built on the same spot. A long period when the site was uninhabited followed. Then, around 2500 BCE, several new palaces were built nearby. A ziggurat (stepped pyramid), dating to around 2000 BCE, was excavated at the shallowest layer of the site. Archaeologists also uncovered a residential area close to the temple and a large cemetery.

Artifacts

In the same part of the site as the residential area and the cemetery, archaeologists found

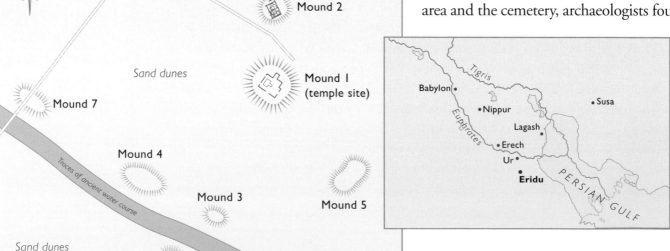

▲ A plan of the settlement at Eridu, showing the various archaeological sites. Inset: the position of Eridu in western Asia.

a quantity of potsherds of cups, bowls, plates, and spouted vessels dating from around 4000 BCE. The pottery is of a high quality and may indicate the early emergence of class divisions, with an elite group using superior pottery and building more sophisticated temples. Some of the cemetery plots contained precious objects, such as beads of obsidian, that were not locally available, a fact that suggests the people of Eridu had contact with other cities. Also found was a clay model of a sailing boat, the earliest evidence of water transport in any ancient civilization.

SEE ALSO

• Mesopotamia • Sumer

▼ *These mud huts of marsh dwellers, living on floating reed islands in southern Iraq, were built using techniques similar to those of ancient Eridu.*

ADAPA

A traditional Mesopotamian story tells of Adapa, a wise man and priest who served the shrine of Ea in the city of Eridu. One day, while Adapa was out fishing, a strong wind overturned his boat, and in his annoyance Adapa cursed the wind and caused it to cease blowing. Adapa was called before the sky god to face his punishment for this act. However, he was forewarned by Ea, who instructed him how to win over the sky god and gain forgiveness. The sky god not only forgave Adapa but also offered him immortality if he accepted the "water and food of life." Ea had warned Adapa not to accept such a gift. The sky god broke into "divine laughter" when his gift was refused, and he allowed Adapa to return to earth.

The gift of immortality may have been a trick that Ea saved Adapa from. On the other hand, Ea may have been jealous of the idea of Adapa becoming immortal and for this reason warned him not to accept the offer of water and food. Either way, the moral of the story is that a man cannot achieve immortality and become like a god.

Etruscans

The Etruscans were an ancient people who lived in Italy between the Tiber and Arno Rivers, west and south of the Apennine Mountains. Their civilization began in the eighth century BCE and lasted until the first century BCE. They developed some of the first towns in Italy and were at their most powerful in the sixth century BCE. For a century or more they were the most powerful civilization on the Italian peninsula, and they heavily influenced the Romans in many aspects of their culture, including architecture, engineering, clothing, games, numbers, religion, art, and elements of theater.

A map showing the Etruscan area of influence, the cities in the Etruscan league, and the other peoples of the region in 500 BCE.

The Etruscan Empire

The Etruscan civilization developed in the seventh century BCE in the northwest central area of the Italian peninsula. The Etruscans found deposits of metal ore that they mined and turned into artifacts to trade. Small villages developed into towns, and they began trading farther afield. Soon they came into competition with the Greeks who were establishing colonies in southern Italy. By the sixth century BCE the Etruscans were pushing northward and had extended their empire along the Adriatic coastline to modern-day Ravenna, Rimini, and Spina. From the edges of their empire, they traded with cities in central Europe, with Greek colonies in Istria, and beyond.

In the seventh century BCE the area that was to become Rome was a series of scattered villages. The Etruscans combined these villages into a whole community. One group of Etruscans, the Tarquins, were said to have ruled Rome from 616 until 509 BCE, when they were finally driven out and the Roman Republic was established.

The fifth century BCE saw the gradual decline of the Etruscan Empire. The Tarquins were expelled from Rome, and Etruscan fleets lost sea battles in the Mediterranean. By the fourth century BCE Rome had conquered Etruscan city-states in the south, while the Celts invaded from the north. During the third century BCE the Etruscans gradually became absorbed into the territory ruled by Rome.

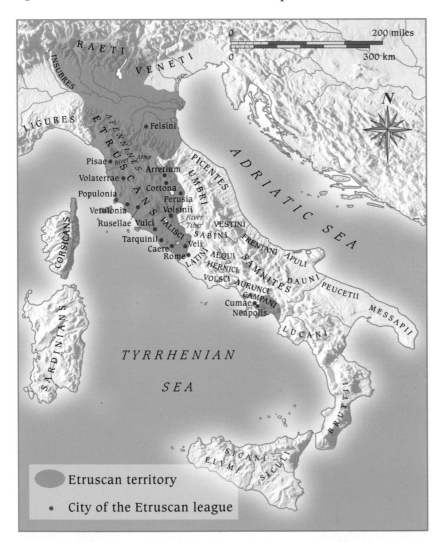

Etruscan territory

City of the Etruscan league

TARQUIN

c. 550–495 BCE

The most famous Etruscan was Tarquinius Superbus, the tyrannical ruler of ancient Rome. All that is known about Tarquin has come through Roman historians writing several centuries later, so it is possible that the stories about him are invented. However, according to legend Tarquin murdered his own father-in-law in order to take power in Rome; he also murdered many senators who tried to oppose him and forced the people of Rome to do hard, unpaid labor on public buildings. After his son attacked a noblewoman called Lucretia, he and his family were driven out of the city, and the Roman Republic was established.

ETRUSCANS

700–600 BCE

Etruscans develop writing and the pottery wheel.

616 BCE

The Tarquin family begins to rule Rome.

600–500 BCE

Emergence of powerful city-states. Almost all of Italy comes under Etruscan control.

509 BCE

The Tarquins are expelled from Rome.

474 BCE

Etruscan fleet is destroyed off Cumae by ships of Hieron I of Syracuse.

390 BCE

Northern Celtic tribes attack Rome.

c. 350 BCE

Celtic tribes move into northern Etruscan territories as far as the Po valley.

250 BCE

Surviving Etruscan city-states come under Roman control.

90 BCE

Roman citizenship is granted to all Italic people. Etruscans become part of the Roman Republic.

41 CE

Etruscan language has completely disappeared from Italy.

▼ This sarcophagus, a terra-cotta coffin, was made for an Etruscan woman called Larthia Seinti in the second century BCE. She was probably very wealthy and wore Roman-style clothing.

Religion

The Etruscans worshiped about forty gods, led by Tinia, the equivalent of Jupiter in Roman religion. Tinia's wife was Uni, and his brother was Sethlans, the equivalent of the Roman god Vulcan. A very popular goddess was Menvra, the goddess of marriage and childbirth.

It was the job of priests, called haruspices, to discover what the gods wanted. These men looked at the internal organs of sacrificial animals, the pattern of birds in the sky, or an unusual event such as an earthquake. They interpreted what they saw as messages from the gods.

Culture

The Etruscans lived in small city-states surrounded by farms worked on by people who lived in the city. Early houses were round with a cone-shaped roof, but later ones were rectangular and were built around a central courtyard. Etruscans also built grand public buildings, such as temples, which were raised on a stone platform but built of wood and brick. The temples were decorated with pottery statues and sculptures. The Etruscans discovered how to build arches, a skill they passed on to the Romans.

The Etruscans made swords, jewelry, tools, mirrors, and chariots out of metal, particularly bronze. Although they had an alphabet and their own language, very little evidence of Etruscan writing has survived. Most of what remains is in the form of inscriptions on graves. Curiously, a piece of Etruscan script was found on a fragment of recycled linen that had been torn into strips and wrapped around a mummy in Egypt.

The Etruscans traded widely and had access to the ideas and inventions of the Greeks and Phoenicians. They drove their goods overland in wheeled carts and had sophisticated ships. They wore both draped clothes, like the Roman toga, and fitted and sewn clothes. Women took an active part in society – many grave paintings show scenes of women involved in farming, games, parties, and religious and sporting festivals. Wealthy Etruscans kept slaves, who did most of their domestic work, but stories tell of some Etruscan slaves owning their own homes and living very comfortable lives.

Archaeology

Because Etruscan homes were made of brick and wood, rather than stone, very little remains of them. However, in several places the grid plan of the city can still be traced, as can the foundations and pottery decorations of some of their temples.

Most of the information, however, comes from the necropolises (cemeteries), where the carved stone gives an idea of what Etruscan windows, doors, furniture, and houses looked like. Grave goods that have been found include beautiful jewelry, bronze mirrors and tools, and many everyday items. The insides of the tombs were often painted, and these paintings give an idea of daily life, with scenes from the working day, paintings of festivals, and carefully painted figures, perhaps of the tomb's owner.

SEE ALSO

- Celts • Greece, Classical • Phoenicians
- Roman Republic and Empire

NECROPOLIS

The Etruscans believed in an afterlife where the dead person would need many material goods. These were buried in the tomb with the dead body. Most Etruscan towns had a necropolis – literally, a "city of the dead," made up entirely of tombs. The tombs in the necropolis were laid out in a formal way, like houses in a town, with "streets" running between them. The tombs were mostly above the ground. They were carved out of rock with carved windows and furniture and painted scenes telling the story of the funeral.

▲ *Inside an Etruscan necropolis at Caere in Tuscany. The pillars and niches are highly decorated, and when the tomb was first built, it would have been filled with all the things that the dead person needed for the next life.*

Families

People in many ancient cultures lived in large family groups with relatives of different ages in the same household. This arrangement was the best way of protecting family property and making sure that all the work of the household was done. It also ensured that there were people available to look after infants and tend the sick and elderly.

In cultures as different as China and Rome, the wider clan of related families was important. In China the clan was known as the *tsu*, while in Rome it was called the *gens*. An important leader in a Roman or Chinese clan was expected to provide money to help educate and marry off clan members who came from poorer families.

Head of the Family

Fathers in ancient times had great power over their families. In several ancient cultures the father not only protected the rest of the group but also acted as a priest in the family's religious ceremonies. The eldest son of a Roman citizen became paterfamilias, or head of the household, on the death of his father, and all family members had to respect his decisions.

In ancient India fathers also had great authority over all the relatives who lived in the household. However, in some parts of India, a father stood down as head of the household once his eldest son was married. The aging father then left his home to live the life of a hermit.

▶ Much of the power that fathers enjoyed came from the leading role that they played in the religious life of the family. In this fourth-century-BCE relief, a Greek father prepares to sacrifice a ram to the god Dionysus while the rest of his family looks on.

282 Families

Greek fathers expected total obedience from their families. In some Greek cities fathers could even sell family members into slavery to pay off debts. Like the Greeks, ancient Hebrew fathers were absolute masters of their families and had the right of life and death over their children. The Hebrew phrase "house of the father" was often used to describe the whole family unit of wives, children, and servants.

Belonging to a Family

Most ancient cultures had rules about how families were organized. In ancient China the extended family worked together as a team at the family trade or in the fields. All food and money that the family earned was shared. When Chinese sons grew up and married, they stayed in their father's house. Only daughters left home and went to live with their in-laws when they married, joining their husband's family. A Mayan bridegroom left his family and built a new house next to his in-laws. He had to work for his father-in-law for an agreed number of years to pay the bride price.

ANCESTOR WORSHIP

In many ancient societies, families revered their ancestors. Mayan families placed the bodies of their dead forefathers under the floor of the main room in the family house. The Romans believed that the manes, *or souls of departed relatives, remained around the household watching over the family. Food and other gifts were left in the family shrine for the* manes *every morning.*

In ancient China the names of family ancestors were written on narrow tablets of seasoned wood. These were hung in a special room in the house to remind the living family of the debt they owed to their dead relatives. Chinese families made sure that the graves of their ancestors were carefully tended. The young were taught that, if they misbehaved, they would bring shame to the family ancestors.

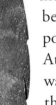

Ancient Hebrew families included slaves, concubines, or secondary wives, and hired servants, as well as blood relatives and in-laws. Everyone banded together for safety and accepted the rule of the father figure.

The Family and the State

Ancient rulers often took an interest in the families that they ruled, sometimes because they feared the power of important clans. At other times rulers wanted to use families for their own ends. The Roman emperor Augustus wanted to make sure that Roman parents had large families, as he needed a constant supply of men for the army. He passed several laws to encourage childbearing. Roman mothers who had three or more children were granted special privileges and rewards by the state, while unmarried men and women had to pay higher taxes and lost half of their inheritance.

▲ The family was the foundation stone of Roman society. In public, the ruling families of Rome presented themselves as models of stability and good order, as in this third-century-CE painting of the Emperor Septimius Severus and his family.

The Family Name

Keeping the family name alive was important in several ancient cultures. Most Roman boys had a first name and two others, a family name and a clan name. Thus, Marcus Cornelius Scipio was Marcus of the clan Cornelius of the family Scipio. The Maya gave their children four names. In addition to a first name and a family nickname, every Mayan child carried the family name of his or her mother and father. This method ensured that no one married a close relative.

THE FOLLOWING IS A HEBREW PRAYER FROM THE BOOK OF ECCLESIASTICUS IN THE APOCRYPHA:

With all your heart honor your father,
and do not forget the birth pangs of your mother.
Remember that through your parents you were born,
And what can you give back to them that equals their gift to you?

ECCLESIASTICUS 7:27-28

SEE ALSO

• Children • China • Greece, Classical • Hebrews • Maya
• Men • Roman Republic and Empire • Women

Farming

The cultivation of crops and the rearing of animals are two of the most important steps ever taken by humans. The techniques of farming were first practiced in western Asia during the Neolithic period in the tenth millennium BCE. Farming developed a little later in other parts of the world, including China and Mexico.

The First Farmers

Before farming, people lived nomadic lives, wandering from place to place as they gathered wild foods and hunted animals. The development of farming allowed people to settle in one place and build villages, which eventually developed into towns.

During the tenth millennium BCE farming developed in several parts of western Asia and north Africa, including Mesopotamia (present-day Iraq), Palestine, and Egypt. Later, around 7000 BCE, farmers began growing crops by the Indus River in India, by the Yellow River in eastern China, and in parts of Mexico.

Irrigation

The key to farming in most of these areas was the ability to water the land through the digging of artificial channels. This process is known as irrigation. Regions such as Mesopotamia, Egypt, and eastern China were watered by mighty rivers that flooded yearly. The floods spread a layer of rich silt (river mud) over the land and thus made the soil fertile.

In summer, however, little rain fell, and the soil baked dry. The land could be farmed successfully only when humans learned to dig channels to regulate the flow of water. People also built dikes (embankments) and dams to prevent the floods from eroding the land along river banks.

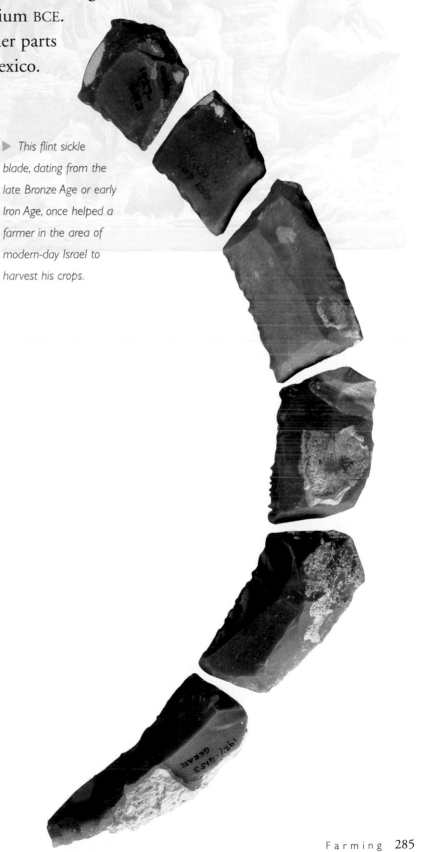

▶ This flint sickle blade, dating from the late Bronze Age or early Iron Age, once helped a farmer in the area of modern-day Israel to harvest his crops.

▲ *This wall painting from an Egyptian tomb shows farmers working in their fields. It dates from the fifteenth century BCE.*

Irrigation made a regular supply of water available through the year. Soon farmers were producing a surplus of food; the surplus allowed some people to leave farmwork and do other jobs instead. Some became weavers or toolmakers; others became soldiers, traders, priests, and administrators. Civilization developed as villages grew into towns and cities.

Grain Crops

Cereals such as wheat, barley, millet, oats, and rice are the world's most important crops because they provide most of the human food supply. The grain (seeds) they produce is stored long after harvest and provides food throughout the year. Early farmers began to cultivate grain crops by saving the seeds of edible plants and sowing them the following year. Gradually, hardy strains of cereals that produced a large quantity of grain developed. In this way the original wild plants slowly developed into modern cereal crops.

In Mesopotamia wheat and barley were grown from the eighth millennium BCE. The harvested grain was stored in special buildings called granaries and was used to feed the cities that grew up along the Tigris and Euphrates Rivers. In China millet and rice were cultivated from the sixth millennium BCE. Rice must be grown on level ground in flooded fields called paddies. Chinese farmers gradually brought more land under cultivation by cutting sloping hillsides into terraces, or steps.

Fruit and Vegetables

From early times farmers also grew other crops, including fruits and vegetables. Mesopotamian farmers grew onions, melons, cucumbers, dates, and figs, as well as cereal crops. Indian farmers grew cotton. Flax, another ancient crop, was grown for its fibers, which were used to make textiles.

In Mexico squash was grown from about 8000 BCE. Egyptian farmers cultivated many different crops, including vines to make wine from around 3000 BCE. Two thousand years later grapes were also being grown in lands north of the Mediterranean, along with olives, apples, pomegranates, and peaches. In China early crops included cotton and tea.

New Irrigation Techniques

Between 2500 BCE and 500 CE irrigation techniques improved in many parts of the world. By around 2000 BCE large-scale irrigation systems were in use in China and western Asia. Canals linking rivers separated by long distances were laboriously dug by hand; tens of thousands of Chinese and Mesopotamian workers were forced to help with public projects. In Egypt the population was also employed in large-scale irrigation projects.

FARM TOOLS AND MACHINERY

The earliest farm tools were made of stone and wood, lashed together with straw or reeds. They included an axlike tool called an adze and simple digging sticks that later developed into spades and hoes. In Neolithic times stone-bladed sickles were used to harvest grain crops. Simple plows helped break up the soil and prepare it for crops.

The first plows were pulled by people, but by 3000 BCE oxen were being used to pull plows in Egypt and Mesopotamia. Around the same time people learned to make a metal called bronze by heating copper and tin. Around 1000 BCE they learned to make iron, an even tougher metal. Plows tipped with iron and sickles with metal blades were much more effective than stone tools had been.

After 3000 BCE many new farming tools were developed. Mesopotamian farmers began to affix funnels to plows so that they could sow seeds as they turned the soil. Soon farmers of western Asia were using animals to help with the work of threshing, that is, processing the harvested grain.

▼ This bronze Etruscan statue of a plowman and his oxen dates from the the sixth century BCE.

During the third century BCE the Greek scientist Archimedes invented a screw to raise river water to fields at higher levels. Archimedes' screw is still used for irrigation in many parts of the world.

In Egypt, before the introduction of Archimedes' screw, water was raised using a machine called a shadoof. In China human pedalers powered an irrigation machine called an endless wheel. The Romans built aqueducts, laid pipes, and dug channels to carry water long distances to dry regions. Their engineering skill allowed them to grow crops on lands where farming had never been possible before.

Roman Farmers

Roman civilization began before 500 BCE as a society of small, independent farms in Italy. By 200 CE the Roman Empire covered much of Europe, North Africa, and western Asia. As the empire grew, small Roman farms developed into large estates. Most estates were owned by rich landlords who lived in faraway cities. The estates were worked by slaves, who were supervised by paid overseers. Many of these slaves had been captured in war.

Many Roman farms specialized in growing wheat to supply grain to the cities of the empire. The Romans transported seeds of productive crops throughout the empire and also established plantations of useful trees. They introduced the ox-drawn plow to Europe and built huge granaries. In addition, Roman scholars wrote long works about the theory of farming.

Roman farmers also pioneered new farming methods, including the practice of leaving fields fallow (unplanted) every other year, a practice that makes the soil more fertile. They developed the technique of crop rotation, that is, planting different crops on the same plot of land in a three- or four-year cycle. Crop rotation produces higher yields.

Goddesses of Farming

All over the world people worshiped earth deities, usually goddesses, who were believed to help farmers by allowing crops to flourish. Farming families prayed and sometimes made sacrifices to the goddess to bring good harvests. In ancient Greece the earth goddess was called Gaea. She was one of the earliest Greek deities. The Greek poet Homer writes, "I shall sing of Gaea, the universal mother, firmly founded, the oldest of divinities." In Egypt the god of resurrection, Osiris, was also associated with the growth of crops, as were a range of goddesses, such as the snake goddess Renenutet.

▼ *A modern farmer uses the screw invented by the Greek scientist Archimedes to raise water from a river for irrigation.*

REARING ANIMALS

The domestication of animals began in many parts of the world about the same time as crop farming. People began to keep herds of useful animals such as cattle, sheep, and horses for their meat, milk, hides, and wool. They probably captured wild animals when young and tamed them. They then selected the beasts that produced the most meat or milk or yielded the finest wool for breeding. In this way wild species gradually developed into productive tame breeds.

By dating animal remains, experts have learned that sheep were being reared in Mesopotamia eleven thousand years ago and asses two thousand years later. In Persia (present-day Iran) goats were kept from 8000 BCE, cattle from 5000 BCE. In Asia nomadic herdsmen bred horses and camels. Pigs were reared in Thailand and China. In the Andes Mountains in South America, llama and alpaca were reared for their warm wool and meat; guinea pigs were also kept for their meat. Domestic animals included chicks, ducks, geese, cats, and dogs.

▼ This Roman statue from Carthage in North Africa shows the earth goddess, who was believed to bring fertility to the land.

The Greeks held a festival of flowers, Anthesteries, in spring. It lasted for three days, and during the festivities people opened jars of new wine and offered the first drops to the gods. The Greeks also celebrated their own first fruits festival in late May. It was called Thargelia and was dedicated to the god Apollo.

▼ This statue of the goddess Demeter was probably carved by the sculptor Lechares around 330 BCE. It was found in Cnidus, Greece.

Harvest Festivals

Harvest festivals were celebrated during the autumn in many parts of the ancient world to ask the gods to provide the community with plentiful food or to thank them for what they have given. The Greeks celebrated Thesmosphoria in the autumn, which was held in honor of Demeter, the goddess of grain. Worshipers made offerings of seeds, cakes, fruits, and animals, praying that Demeter would grant them a good harvest.

In the Hebrew harvest festival of Sukkoth, the ancient Jews hung fruits and vegetables inside makeshift huts to thank God for his bounty. The Egyptians held one of their harvest festivals in honor of Min, a god of fertility and vegetation. During a long ritual, arrows were shot toward the four points of the compass, and birds were released from cages and encouraged to fly north, south, east, and west. The ritual represented the harmony of people with nature.

Farmers in ancient Britain believed that the spirit of the corn lived in the fields, trapped in the last sheaf of corn, and so people did not crush these ears of wheat. Instead, they used them to make corn dolls, small, humanlike figures, which they placed in a bonfire to release the spirit. The practice still exists.

Days of the Dead

The ancient Celts in England, Scotland, and Ireland celebrated the end of the year on October 31, when the farmers brought their flocks of sheep down from the hills, where they had been grazing all summer. During the festival, called Samhain, people lit bonfires to scare away the ghosts of the dead, which were believed to return home for a night on

CHRISTIAN FESTIVALS

The leaders of the early Christian Church tried to ban pagan festivals. When people refused to give up these ancient practices, early popes and bishops superimposed Christian celebrations on pagan festivals.

The spring festival became Easter, commemorating the day Jesus rose from the dead. Christians believed that the resurrection of Jesus brought new life to the world, and so symbols of rebirth, such as the egg, were kept by Christians and are still used. The Saturnalia, a Roman midwinter celebration, was transformed into Christmas, commemorating the birth of Jesus. Similarly, harvest festivals became days when Christians thanked God for his generosity.

In the ninth century CE the Celtic festival of Samhain was changed into All Saints Day, or All Hallows Day, a day for celebrating the lives of the saints (November 1). October 31, All Hallows Eve, or Halloween, is still a festive day for children.

November 1st, the beginning of the Celtic New Year. The Celts offered sacrifices to the gods to urge them to keep the dead and other monsters away.

The ancient Maya, whose culture flourished in Central America between 250 and 900 CE, held festivals in honor of the dead. During special ceremonies they invoked the spirits of dead relatives to ask for their advice. The festival was held at regular intervals during the year, known as ahau days.

▼ Jewish people still celebrate the festival of Sukkoth. The festivities last for seven days. Special huts are put up in the synagogues and in people's gardens. Families gather in them to eat their meals.

Food and Drink

The first humans were vegetarians; they ate wild fruits, roots, and berries. Around 400,000 years ago, humans began cooking and eating animal meat. The Neanderthals, who first appeared in Europe some 110,000 years ago, hunted and ate a variety of animals, including bears, woolly rhinoceroses, wild horses, deer, ibex, reindeer, and – when people were on the move – hare and wildfowl. Neanderthals roasted meat over open fires. By 8000 BCE the people of Neolithic Japan were cooking and storing food in earthenware cooking pots.

▼ This model of two bakers from ancient Egypt was found in a tomb. One of the bakers is grinding corn while the other one is baking the bread at an oven. The Egyptians made all sorts of breads, including flat pitas and fancy loaves shaped like people and animals.

Bread

Bread, the staple food of many ancient people, was first baked in 10,000 BCE. Flour was made by crushing wheat between two stones. The rough grain was mixed with water to make dough. The loaves were probably placed on flat stones and baked under hot ashes. This early form of flat

bread was coarse and unpleasant to eat and became stale very quickly. Over time the Egyptians discovered that fermenting the dough before baking it made the bread rise. The Egyptians were also the first to bake bread in an oven.

Egyptian Food

In ancient Egypt wheat was used to make both bread and a thick sort of beer that looked rather like soup. It was often drunk through a straw with a small filter. The fertile land around the Nile yielded such vegetables as leeks, onions, garlic, beans, and lettuce. For dessert people ate small round cakes or fruit such as melon and figs. The Egyptians did not have sugar, so they sweetened their food with honey and dates.

Because there was little land for grazing, meat was expensive. While wealthy Egyptians feasted on beef, goose, and duck, poorer households ate mainly bread and vegetables and any animals they could catch when hunting. Fish were also available from the Nile and were often salted to preserve them longer. Although the rich usually drank wine and often imported fine wines from Syria, most people drank beer, even children.

Greek Food

The staple diet of the Greeks was bread, goat's cheese, and olives. They imported the wheat from Egypt to make their bread, which they baked in small, portable ovens filled with hot ashes. The Greeks also cooked a variety of fish, including mackerel, tuna, squid, octopus, and prickly sea urchins. Meat was a rare treat, reserved for festivals, when people would sacrifice animals to the gods.

Greek people cooked most of their meals at the hearth. They liked stews and

food fried in olive oil. Fish dishes were flavored with easily grown herbs such as bay leaves, rosemary, and thyme. Cakes were baked with honey. They also ate a lot of sweet fruits, including figs and pomegranates, and they dried grapes in the sun to make raisins.

▲ A detail from a fifth century-BCE vase shows two Greeks taking part in a banquet.

PART OF A HYMN TO NINKASI, THE SUMERIAN GODDESS OF BEER, FOUND ON A TABLET FROM THE NINETEENTH CENTURY BCE:

When you pour out the filtered beer
of the collector vat
It is like the rushing of
the Tigris and the Euphrates
Ninkasi, you are the one who pours out
the filtered beer

A scene from a Roman banquet found in the ruins of Pompeii. To the left, a slave is removing a guest's sandal so he can bathe his feet. Another slave offers the guest some refreshment.

Etruscan Food

The Etruscans grew a wide variety of cereals, vegetables, and fruit. They caught tuna and collected tortoise eggs. Popular meals included fish stuffed with rosemary, roasted pork, and pig's liver cooked with bay leaves. Beef, venison, hare, and duck were also eaten, served with sauces and gravies. The Etruscans had beautiful table manners. They ate with their hands, cleaning them with soft bread when they finished and washing their fingers in bowls of scented water. There were two meals a day, which rich people ate sitting on chairs or, toward the end of the sixth century BCE, reclining on couches.

Roman Food

At dawn the Romans ate a simple breakfast called the *ientaclum*, made up of leftovers from the day before together with milk and bread. This meal was followed by *prandium*, a simple lunch usually bought from a street vendor, perhaps on the way to the baths or while at work.

Dinner, or *cena*, eaten at sunset, was an elaborate meal for the rich. Sometimes friends were invited in for a *convivium* (banquet). Popular Roman delicacies included dormice stuffed with poppy seeds, snails, minced lobster balls, and oysters.

Roman cooks used spices brought to Rome from the farthest reaches of the empire or from the east. They included pepper, clove, saffron, and fennel. The Romans loved sauces, too. One of the most common was *garum* sauce. It was made with anchovy paste and grape juice.

Poor people in Rome lived in small apartments, and many did not have facilities for cooking. They bought their food from street or market stalls. Roman soldiers carried ovens with them to make bread and cook food. Sometimes they were paid in salt. This pay was known as *salarium*, from which the modern word *salary* comes.

DRINK

The Sumerians were perhaps the first people to brew beer. Around 4000 BCE they were making a cloudy sort of ale by leaving cakes of emmer wheat to ferment in water. In the third millennium BCE the Mesopotamians learned how to make a stronger brew by germinating and drying the grain. In ancient Babylon both men and women drank beer. It was considered such an important part of life that tavern keepers who cheated their customers were drowned. The Egyptians liked beer, too, while the Greeks and the Romans preferred wine. The Romans considered ale a drink fit only for savages and barbarians.

Wine was first made in the Zagros Mountains of Mesopotamia around 5200 BCE. The Greeks, who considered wine sacred, even had a god of wine, named Dionysus. According to legend Dionysus had escaped from Mesopotamia because people there preferred beer. The Greeks always drank wine mixed with water. The Romans planted vines all over their empire, introducing them to France, where wine making became an important part of the economy.

Milk has been a popular beverage since 9000 BCE, when people first started to milk goats, sheep, horses, and donkeys. Tea, which is made from a plant native to Southeast Asia, was being drunk in China by 350 CE. Although tea did not come to Europe until the sixteenth century CE, it has since become one of the most popular drinks in the world.

▶ This statue of Bacchus, the Roman god of wine, was found in a temple on the Janiculum Hill in Rome. It is a copy of a Greek statue showing the god Dioynsus, the Greek god of wine and festivities.

SEE ALSO

Franks

The Franks were a Germanic people who lived along the banks of the Rhine. The name Frank probably came from the Old German *frak* or *frech,* which means "fierce" or "proud." Over time the Latin version, Franci, came to mean "freemen." Both the country of France and the German province of Franconia are named after this powerful people.

Conquering Gaul

The Franks began to raid Roman Gaul in the years after 275 CE. Frankish tribes had settled in what is now Belgium and the Netherlands by 320. By 450 there were many Frankish settlements across northern Gaul. In the later fifth century King Childeric (died 481) and his son Clovis united the Frankish tribes into one nation. Clovis defeated the Visigoths in the south, and one of his sons defeated the Burgundians, another Germanic tribe. By 540 the kingdom of the Franks extended across almost all of modern-day France.

Allies of Rome

Between 300 and 450 CE many Franks were allies of Rome. Their tribal leaders often adopted Roman fashions, learned Latin, and held high office in the late Roman Empire. The emperor Magnentius (reigned 350–353), in fact, had a Frankish mother, and in the mid-fourth century the defense of the empire's northern frontier on the Rhine River was in the hands of a Frankish general named Silvanus.

Pagans and Warriors

The Franks were pagans who held on to their old tribal customs. Some Frankish tribes mutilated and beheaded their dead before burial. Horses were sometimes slaughtered and placed in the grave of an important chieftain. The Franks were fierce warriors. Unlike some barbarian peoples who fought on horseback, the Franks preferred to fight on foot. Their favorite weapon was the *francisca,* or heavy throwing ax. Frankish warriors charged into battle, throwing their axes as they closed on the enemy. They fought with a short, sharp sword called the *scramasax.*

▼ A map showing the position of the kingdom of the Franks in Europe around 500 CE.

0   1000 miles
0   1600 km

N

ATLANTIC OCEAN

NORTH SEA

BALTIC SEA

BRITONS

ANGLO SAXONS

SAXONS

S L A V S

Elbe

KINGDOM OF THE FRANKS

Loire

Rhine

LOMBARDS

BURGUNDIANS

KINGDOM OF THE OSTROGOTHS

Danube

SUEVI

KINGDOM OF THE VISIGOTHS

KINGDOM OF THE VANDALS

Constantinople

EASTERN ROMAN EMPIRE

M E D I T E R R A N E A N   S E A

🔴 Kingdom of the Franks 500 CE

➤ Movement of the Franks

FRANKS

c. 274 CE

Franks first mentioned in Roman sources.

275 CE

Franks raid Roman Gaul.

350–353 CE

Reign of Roman emperor Magnentius, whose mother was Frankish.

356 CE

The Roman general Julian defeats the Franks near Cologne.

463 CE

The warlord Childeric begins to unite the Franks into one kingdom.

c. 490 CE

Paris becomes the capital of the Frankish kingdom, and the Franks begin the process of Christianization.

496 CE

Franks become Christian.

507 CE

Franks capture southeastern France from the Visigoths.

534 CE

Franks capture southwestern France from the Burgundians.

◀ *This medieval statue of the Frankish King Clovis I stands at the Church of St. Denis in Paris, where many kings of France were buried.*

CLOVIS *465–511 CE*

Clovis (or Chlodwig) was the most energetic of the early Frankish kings. A gifted soldier, he conquered the last Roman province in Gaul in 486 CE. To control his new lands, Clovis made Paris his capital. In 507 he defeated the Visigoths and extended his rule as far south as Toulouse.

In 493 Clovis married a princess from Burgundy, who later became Saint Clotilda. She encouraged Clovis to become a Christian, and after a crushing victory over the Alemanni tribes near Cologne, Clovis and two thousand of his men were baptized on Christmas Day in 496. Clovis is revered as the founder of the kingdom of France. His descendants, the Merovingians, would rule France until 751.

SEE ALSO

• Attila • Constantine • Goths • Huns
• Roman Republic and Empire

Games

Since prehistoric times, people have played games – playful contests involving mental or physical skill. In ancient times, as now, most games were played according to set rules. Many games required equipment such as dice and counters or bats and balls.

Sports are physical games played by teams or individuals competing against one another. Ancient people played sports and games for fun, relaxation, or for a challenge. In some societies, sports and games had a more serious meaning. For example, in ancient Greece the Olympic Games and other organized competitions were held on religious festivals, as sometimes also happened in ancient Egypt. In a few civilizations, including the Olmecs of Central America, games were taken so seriously that the losing side was killed.

Games of Skill

As well as physical sports, adults and children around the world also played less active games, including games of skill and board games. Knucklebones is a game of skill similar to the modern game of jacks. Players tossed small sheep bones into the air and caught them on the backs of their hands. In ancient Rome knucklebones was called *astragali*. In Greece it was very popular among women. Marbles was another game of skill played in many countries, including Greece, Rome, and Egypt.

▶ A Greek statue of two women playing knucklebones, dating from around 340–330 BCE.

In Rome players rolled glass or pottery marbles along the ground onto a marked board or even tossed them into jars.

Board Games

Board games have been played for at least 4,500 years. One of the oldest game boards yet discovered dates back to 2500 BCE. It was found in the city of Ur in Mesopotamia (present-day Iraq). Like many board games, it seems to have been a race game, similar to modern backgammon. Players probably took turns to throw a die and race their counters (game pieces) to the finish.

In ancient Ur and elsewhere board games often involved an element of luck, introduced by tossing dice or marked sticks. Dice made of bone, pottery, or seeds have been found in many different places, including Greece, Egypt, and Rome. Some dice games involved gambling. Roman dice have been found weighted with lead so that a certain number would come up more often. The Romans enjoyed gambling so much that eventually it was banned, except during the winter festival of Saturnalia when the rule was relaxed.

In ancient Egypt two board games, the snake game and *senet*, were very popular. In the snake game, players took turns moving their counters around a board shaped like a coiled serpent. The winner was the first player to reach the snake's head in the middle. In *senet*, players raced each other to the kingdom of the god Osiris around a square board marked with symbols. Lucky players landed on squares representing useful qualities, such as power and beauty. Unlucky players landed on dangers, such as fierce hippos. Four beautifully made *senet* boards were found in the tomb of the young pharaoh Tutankhamen, which was discovered in 1922.

In China the game of go, or *weiqi*, has been played for at least two thousand years. It is played on a square board with two sets of counters. Players try to capture as much territory as possible by surrounding it with their counters. The game requires the ability to plan several moves ahead.

▼ This Egyptian wall painting, from the tomb of the Egyptian queen Nefertari, shows the queen playing senet.

TOYS

Children from many different ancient civilizations had fun with toys. Similar toys that seem to be loved almost everywhere include dolls, toy animals, puzzles, and balls. Dolls made from clay, wood, hide, rags, and even metal have been found in many regions, as well as in the tombs of Greek, Roman, and Egyptian children. In ancient times dolls' hair was made of beads, string, or animal hair, sewn on with thread or sinew. Dolls with movable arms and legs date back to about 600 CE.

Pull toys such as carts and animals on wheels have also been found in many different places, including the Indus valley in India. In ancient Egypt toys with moving parts such as jaws and tails were enjoyed by children. Egyptian finds also include a lion whose jaws snap shut when the child pulled on a string and a mouse with a quivering tail. In Rome the children of the wealthy might be given a miniature chariot to ride in. These toy chariots were pulled by donkeys or goats.

▲ These toys of a lion, bird, and hedgehog were made by the Elamites in western Asia around 1150 BCE.

In Africa and parts of Asia, another strategy game, *mancala*, was played on a wooden board carved with little hollows. Players moved their shell or seed counters between the hollows to capture their opponent's pieces.

Children's Games

Around the world children played many different games, including tag, leapfrog, and ball games. Guessing games and riddles were also popular. Egyptian children spun tops and played throwing and catching games, including some on piggyback. Roman children played games similar to ticktacktoe, hopscotch, and hide-and-seek.

SEE ALSO
- Children • China • Egypt • Greece, Classical • Indus Valley
- Mesopotamia • Olmecs • Plato • Roman Republic and Empire
- Sports and Entertainment • Tutankhamen • Ur

Geography

Geography is the scientific study of the earth's surface and its influence on living things, including people. The word *geography* comes from a Greek term meaning "description of the earth." In ancient times Greek thinkers used mathematics to work out ideas about the earth's size, shape, and nature. On a more practical level, many ancient peoples developed surveying techniques that helped them to measure the size of their fields and properties. Travelers from many different countries recorded geographical information on maps.

Maps

From early times, soldiers, traders, and other travelers visiting unknown territory made maps to record the details of their journeys. Maps were made by civilizations all over the ancient world, even by peoples with no written language.

The earliest known map is a Babylonian clay tablet dating from about 2300 BCE. It shows part of the city-state of Akkad.

Streams, settlements, and hills are all marked on the map, along with three compass points, north, east, and west. The Babylonians were skilled astronomers and mathematicians. They were the first people to divide a circle into 360 equal parts, or degrees. This innovation later helped Greek geographers develop the system of latitude and longitude to plot and measure distances on maps.

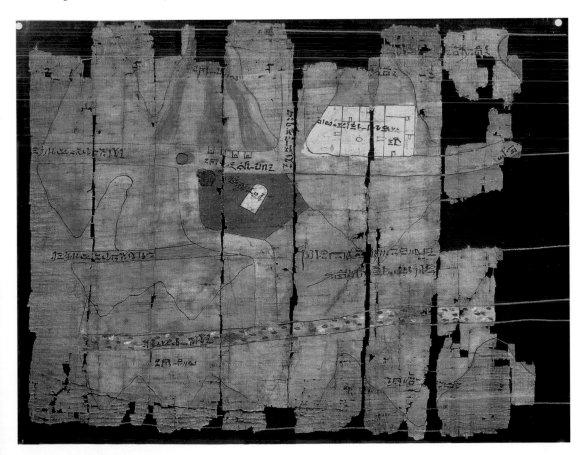

◄ This map was made by Egyptian mapmakers in about 1150 BCE. It shows the quarries of Wadi Hammamat in the Eastern Desert.

▲ *The Greek geographer and mapmaker Eratosthenes, as portrayed in a seventeenth-century engraving.*

By the second millennium BCE the Egyptians, Phoenicians, and other Mediterranean peoples were exploring the lands of Europe and North Africa with the aim of trade or conquest. Their journeys increased ancient knowledge of the known world and were duly recorded on maps. The Egyptians in particular were skilled surveyors and measurers. They used surveying techniques to establish property boundaries along the Nile River, which flooded regularly, washing away field markers. As early as 1300 BCE the Egyptians were drawing accurate maps.

In China during the Han era (200s BCE–200s CE), several emperors ordered military expeditions to explore, conquer, and map remote lands to the west. By the second century BCE the Chinese were drawing maps on silk cloth woven with a grid of faint lines that helped indicate direction and the distance between towns. Several of these ancient maps survive.

Understanding the Earth

Before the Greeks early civilizations had believed that the earth was flat. In the sixth century BCE the Greek mathematician Pythagoras was among the first to suggest that the earth was round. In the same century a Greek scholar named Anaximander (610–c. 546 BCE) is thought to have produced the first known world map, showing Greek lands at the center, surrounded by ocean. Anaximander's map was circular in shape.

Two hundred years later the Greek philosopher Aristotle (384–322 BCE) argued the case for the round-earth theory. He supported his argument with a wealth of scientific detail, including the observation that the earth cast a round shadow on the moon during a lunar eclipse.

In the third century BCE the Greek astronomer and philosopher Eratosthenes of Alexandria (c. 276–c. 194 BCE) used geometry and observations regarding the sun's angle at the summer solstice in different places to work out the circumference of the earth. His calculation was remarkably accurate, being off by only 50 miles (80 km). Eratosthenes was among the first to use the term *geographia* to describe writings about the earth. He also produced a new, detailed map of the known world, extending from Britain in the west to the Indian Ganges River in the east and Libya in North Africa in the south.

Geographers of Greece and Rome

The Greeks were the first civilization to study geography systematically. Several Greek writers recorded the observation that the physical geography of a region affected the daily life of the people settled there.

From the third century BCE the Romans increased European knowledge of the

LATITUDE AND LONGITUDE

Latitude and longitude form an imaginary grid of lines that crisscross the earth at regular intervals. Lines of latitude travel east to west, and lines of longitude travel north to south. When shown on maps, they provide a frame of reference that allows map users to calculate direction and the distance between places marked on the map; this system helps them to plan their journeys. It was gradually developed by Greek geographers between the third century BCE and the second century CE.

Eratosthenes' world map from the third century BCE was the first to show regularly spaced east-west lines, which are now called parallels. Around fifty years later, the astronomer Hipparchus added north-south lines, now called meridians, at right angles to the parallels. In his Geographia, Ptolemy used the terms latitude and longitude to describe the grid created by the lines.

▼ This road map of the Roman Empire, known as Peutinger's Tabula, is a twelfth-century copy of a Roman map.

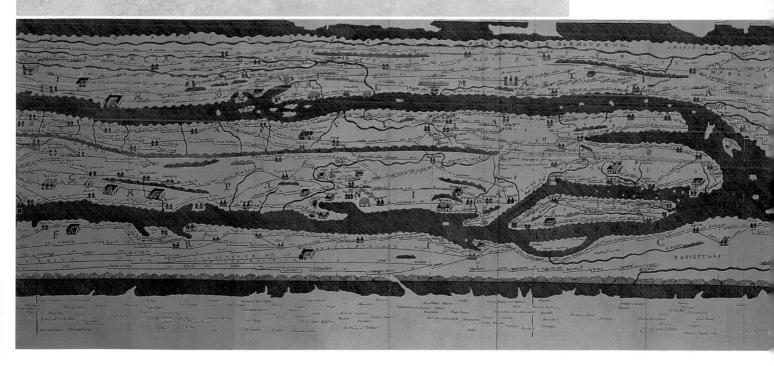

world through conquest and colonization. In the first century BCE the Greek geographer Strabo produced a seventeen-volume work called Geographia, which the Romans used to run their empire.

As well as borrowing Greek ideas, the Romans soon became expert surveyors and mapmakers in their own right. They produced street maps of towns and road maps of their empire.

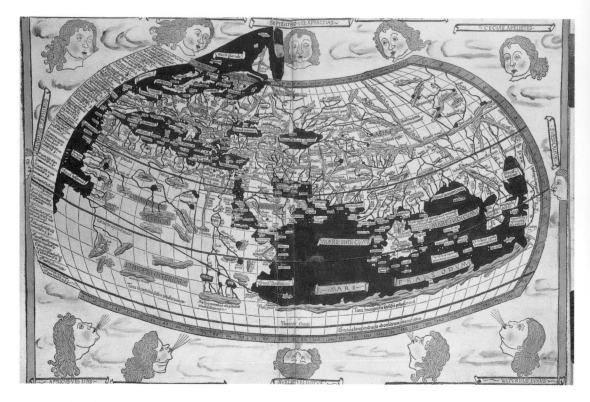

▶ This medieval map of the world was drawn up according to information from Ptolemy's works.

In the first century CE the emperor Augustus Caesar ordered a survey of Roman territories that took twenty years to complete. The results were carved in marble on a master map that stood near the Forum in Rome.

Ptolemy

Ptolemy of Alexandria, a Greek scholar of the second century CE, was a skilled geographer. His eight-volume *Geographia* was a summary of all Greek and Roman knowledge of the subject that had been gathered by that time.

Ptolemy believed that for a map to be useful it must be drawn to an accurate scale. He urged mapmakers to "study the whole in its just proportions." He also wrestled with the difficulty of representing the curving surface of the earth on a flat map. He described different methods of map projection to get around the problem. Ptolemy's *Geographia* included a world map and twenty-six regional maps. Much later it had a huge influence on European map-

makers and explorers during the Renaissance (late 1300s–1600 CE).

In 391 CE, however, a mob wrecked the library at Alexandria, and Egyptian and Greek knowledge of the world was lost to Europeans for centuries. Ptolemy's works survived in Arabic translations, though, and so the Arabs continued to be skilled geographers. After the Roman Empire fell in the fifth century, serious study of geography and accurate mapmaking virtually ceased in Europe for about a thousand years, until Ptolemy's works were translated from the Arabic in the fifteenth century.

> *It may be proved by mathematics that the entire land and water surface of the earth comprises a spherical object that exists around the central point of the heavenly sphere itself.*
>
> PTOLEMY OF ALEXANDRIA, *GEOGRAPHIA*, BOOK 1

Gilgamesh Epic

Gilgamesh is a legendary hero of Mesopotamian literature. His adventures are known largely because they were recorded and preserved on twelve clay tablets in the library of the Assyrian king Ashurbanipal at Nineveh in the seventh century BCE. This account drew on material from three earlier Sumerian poems about Gilgamesh, as well as other sources.

It is possible that Gilgamesh was based on a living king who ruled the city of Erech in southern Mesopotamia between around 3000 and 2500 BCE. Some scholars believe that a king named Gilgamesh ruled in Erech during the first half of the third millennium BCE. It cannot be known for sure, however, whether this is the Gilgamesh of the epic tales.

The Story

The Gilgamesh epic records the tale of a king of Erech — two-thirds god and one third human – who is consumed by a sense of adventure and a love of life. In the first tale a wild man named Enkidu is sent by the god Anu to control the too-powerful Gilgamesh. After a trial of strength, however, Gilgamesh and Enkidu become close friends. They travel to the Cedar Forest, where they ambush and kill the monster Humbaba, the god Ellil's guardian of the Cedar Forest.

Misfortune comes when the goddess of physical love, Ishtar (who is called Inanna in the earlier Sumerian poem), seeks to marry Gilgamesh, only to be rejected by him. In her anger Ishtar sends a bull from heaven to destroy Gilgamesh, but the bull is killed by Enkidu. The good friend of Gilgamesh has to pay with his life for this deed. Gilgamesh suffers the torment of seeing his friend Enkidu die "tearing his hair and scattering the tufts, stripping and flinging down the finery of his body."

▲ These clay tablets from seventh-century-BCE Nineveh tell the Babylonian legend of the flood, part of the Gilgamesh Epic.

Gilgamesh, whither are you wandering?
Life, which you look for, you will never find.
For when the gods created man, they let
death be his share, and life
withheld in their own hands.
Gilgamesh, fill your belly —
day and night make merry,
let days be full of joy,
dance and make music day and night.
And wear fresh clothes,
and wash your head and bathe.
Look at the child that is holding your hand,
and let your wife delight in your embrace.
These things alone are the concern of men.

The hero then sets off on a search for eternal life, but everyone he meets tells him that this journey is hopeless and impossible. He finally meets with someone who is immortal – the survivor of a tremendous flood that had once destroyed the rest of human and animal life. Utnapishtim, the flood survivor, is like the figure of Noah in the biblical Book of Genesis.

In the longest of the tales, Utnapishtim gives a three-hundred-line description of the great flood. He also informs Gilgamesh of the sad fact that no other human can achieve immortality. However, Gilgamesh is told about a magical plant that will restore youth. He finds the plant, but it is eaten by a serpent before Gilgamesh can use it, and he returns, empty-handed and unhappy, to the city of Erech.

SEE ALSO

• Erech • Ishtar • Mesopotamia

▲ *An eighth-century-BCE stone relief from the Palace of Sargon II at Khorsabad, in present-day Iraq, depicting the hero Gilgamesh holding a lion that he had captured.*

Giza

The pyramids at Giza were built as tombs for the pharaohs Khufu (c. 2589–2566 BCE), his son Khafra (c. 2558–2532 BCE), and Khafra's son, Menkaura (c. 2532–2504 BCE). The pyramids were built on a huge scale as a way of displaying the power of the pharaohs.

Scholars believe that the pharaohs were buried with all their treasure and that the pyramid builders tried to protect the tombs from robbers by building thick walls, false passages, and traps. Despite these precautions, all the pyramid tombs at Giza were robbed in ancient times, long before they were excavated by archaeologists.

Pyramid Complexes

Each pyramid is part of a pyramid complex, with temples and smaller tombs built alongside the pyramid for other members of the royal family. Some of the pharaohs even had boats buried next to their pyramids. There are also several cemeteries at Giza for high officials and people who were favorites of the pharaohs.

The Sphinx

The Sphinx is a huge sandstone sculpture of a creature with a lion's body and a man's head, which appears to be guarding Khafra's pyramid. It is 239 feet (73 m) long and 65 feet (20 m) wide. The Sphinx, probably built by Khafra, was carved out of a rock outcrop in front of his pyramid. The face of the Sphinx is believed to be a likeness of Khafra.

Building the Pyramids

Archaeologists believe that the pyramids were built by full-time laborers who worked all year round and lived in a workers' village nearby. These workers included specialist builders and craftsmen as well as manual laborers.

▼ The pyramids at Giza. The Great Pyramid of Khufu is the one on the right. The middle pyramid, Khafra's, seems bigger because Khafra deliberately had it built on higher ground.

▶ *While builders worked on the pyramids, other craftsmen made the possessions for the afterlife that would be placed in the tomb. This tomb painting shows workers painting wooden coffins and making other things to place in the tombs.*

When the River Nile flooded, between July and October, many thousands of farm-workers, who could not work on the land, arrived at Giza. They came to work on the pyramids as part of "duty work" they had to do for the pharaoh. Duty work was something almost everyone in ancient Egypt had to perform for a set number of days each year. It included working on large building projects such as the pyramids. These temporary laborers did much of the heavy work, such as cutting the stone in the nearby quarries and hauling it to the site.

The pyramid builders had very few tools and there is no evidence that they used machinery. They moved the huge blocks of limestone from nearby quarries to Giza by boat when the River Nile was flooded. Any other moving was done by placing the blocks of stone on rollers and hauling them along by rope. While one set of workers pulled on the rope, another group was at work constantly moving the rollers from behind the blocks to the front of them.

The pyramids were built in stepped layers. As the structure rose in height, a mud brick ramp, up which materials could be dragged, was probably built around the pyramid. When the final layers had been completed, the builders filled in the steps with triangular-shaped stone blocks to make a smooth-sided pyramid. The outer surface of the pyramid was then added. It was made from limestone, polished until it shone white and the joints could hardly be seen. The builders made sure the sides were straight and smooth by running a rope coated in red earth over the surface. The rope caught on any bumps, marking them red, and these areas were rubbed away.

The Size of the Pyramids

The biggest pyramid is the Great Pyramid of Khufu. It is about 480 feet (146.5 m) high. The square base covers about thirteen acres (5.25 hectares), or about two hundred tennis courts. It is the largest stone structure ever built. Despite its enormous size the base is an almost perfect square. Each of the four sides is exactly in line with a point of the compass: north, south, east, and west. The Great Pyramid contains over 2,300,000 blocks of stone. Some of these stones are huge, weighing over forty tons (36,280 kg). The average weight of a block is 2.5 tons (2,268 kg).

MASTABA TOMBS

Archaeologists excavating at Giza have also found earlier burials in mastaba tombs. Mastaba means "bench" in Arabic, and mastaba tombs are rectangular buildings beneath which important people were buried. The buildings also housed a chapel dedicated to the dead person. Mastaba tombs were used throughout the period of ancient Egyptian civilization. There may be more royal tombs to be discovered at Giza; the shifting sands make excavation difficult, and archaeologists are still not certain how far the site extends.

The central pyramid, Khafra's, looks bigger than the Great Pyramid because Khafra had it built on higher ground. Khafra's pyramid is about ten feet (3 m) shorter than the Great Pyramid. The smallest of the pyramids, Menkaura's, is just 213 feet (65 m) high. Both later pyramids were carefully sited so that the sides exactly face north, south, east, and west.

SEE ALSO
• Egypt • Pyramids

◄ *The Sphinx at Giza, 239 feet (73 m) long and 65 feet (20 m) wide, was preserved while it was buried in sand. When the sand was removed, the climate and environmental pollution began to damage it. People have been trying different ways to preserve it ever since.*

Goths

The Goths were one of the great migrant peoples of the ancient world. According to Jordanes, a historian of the sixth century CE, their original home was in southern Scandinavia. Although they had some farming skills, the Goths still depended on hunting and gathering for much of their food. As they used up the food in one area, they migrated in search of new supplies.

By around 200 CE, scholars believe, the Goths had reached the edge of the Roman world. They had by this time divided into two separate groups. One had settled in southern Russia and the Ukraine on the rich lands north of the Black Sea. The other had taken over lands to the north of the River Danube in modern-day Romania. This area had been the Roman province of Dacia until 275 CE, when Emperor Aurelian withdrew his legions. These two groups of Goths may later have become the tribes known as the Visigoths and the Ostrogoths.

▼ A map showing the kingdoms of the Visigoths and Ostrogoths in Europe around 500 CE.

The Romans

The Goths made several raids deep into the Roman Empire in the third century CE. In 269 they terrified the Romans at Thessalonika in northern Greece, almost capturing the city with their use of siege machines. It was the first time barbarians had used siege technology so effectively. Other Gothic war bands attacked the rich Roman province of Asia Minor. However, like other barbarian tribes, many of the Gothic raiders soon settled on farmland within the empire and became allies of Rome.

Although there were many more small raids into Roman territory, the Goths lived in peace with Rome for much of the period between 270 and 370. Gothic dukes and warlords often fought on the side of Rome against other barbarian tribes.

Christianity

In the fourth century CE the Goths became Christian. In 325 the teachings of the heretic Christian priest Arius were out-

GOTHS

c. 238 CE

First Gothic raids into the Roman Empire in Danube area.

c. 240–270 CE

Goths raid northern Balkans, Greece, and Asia Minor.

c. 270–370 CE

Goths mostly at peace with Rome.

c. 375 CE

Arrival of the Huns from Asia. Goths flee toward Roman lands.

378 CE

Visigoths defeat the Roman emperor Valens at Adrianople.

410 CE

Visigoths under Alaric sack Rome.

489 CE

Ostrogoths invade Italy.

493 CE

Theodoric sets up successful Ostrogothic kingdom of Italy.

507 CE

Visigoths are defeated by the Franks and lose much of their kingdom in Gaul.

lawed. One of his followers, Ulfilas (c. 311–383 CE), was banished from the Roman lands and went to live among the pagan Goths. Ulfilas converted the Goths to Christianity and translated the Bible into the Gothic language. By 370 the Goths were slowly and peacefully becoming more like their Roman neighbors.

THEODORIC THE GREAT *455–526 CE*

Theodoric was an Ostrogoth prince but was brought up as a Roman at Constantinople. He learned to value the culture and customs of the Roman world. Around 471 he became king of the Ostrogoths and lived in Pannonia (present-day Hungary). In 489 he led his people and an army into Italy. Odoacer, the ruler who had deposed the last western Roman emperor in 476, was defeated in a short war. Although Theodoric pretended to obey the eastern Roman emperor in distant Constantinople, he was really the independent king of Italy. He was a wise king, and his reign brought thirty years of peace and prosperity. His troops were Goths, yet he used Roman governors to run his kingdom, and he treated his Roman and Gothic subjects as equals. Theodoric was an Arian Christian, but he permitted Catholics and Jews to worship in their own way. He made alliances with barbarian kings and the eastern emperor to keep his kingdom at peace.

◀ *Theodoric continued many Roman traditions. This coin shows him in the style of a late Roman emperor.*

The Huns

In the 370s CE the Huns appeared from the steppes of southern Russia. They were a fierce Asian people who swept through eastern Europe conquering and killing. Many Ostrogoths fled westward in panic, perhaps looking for help from Rome or from their western Visigoth cousins. Others were forced to surrender to the Huns and were ruled by them for the next eighty years. After the death of Attila, the Huns' most powerful king, in 453, the Ostrogoths moved into the Balkans and then settled in Italy under Theodoric the Great in 489.

Kingdom of the Visigoths

In 376 the Goths were given permission to enter the Roman Empire. For most of the next century, they acted as a mercenary army for the Romans, although they often fought the Romans for more food, pay, and land. One such battle occurred

in 378; the Goths defeated a Roman army at Adrianople in Thrace, killing the Roman emperor Valens. Under their ruler Alaric the demands of the Goths became increasingly difficult for the Romans to satisfy. The Romans' failure to meet the Gothic demands led Alaric's Goths to sack Rome in 410. A permanent solution was found in 418, when the Visigoths were given lands in southwestern Gaul.

Between 418 and 507 the Visigoths ruled a kingdom in southwestern Gaul centered upon the town of Toulouse. They also expanded into Spain, where they became the dominant military power. At the battle of Vouillé, Clovis, king of the Franks, defeated the Visigoths and drove them out of most of Gaul. The Visigoths remained the rulers of Spain and increased their kingdom over the next century. Visigothic rule in Spain came to an end in 711 with the Islamic conquest.

▶ *Visigothic artists fused their own "barbarian" traditions with the styles they learned from the art of the late Roman Empire. This jeweled bronze fibula, or clasp, was probably made around the year 500.*

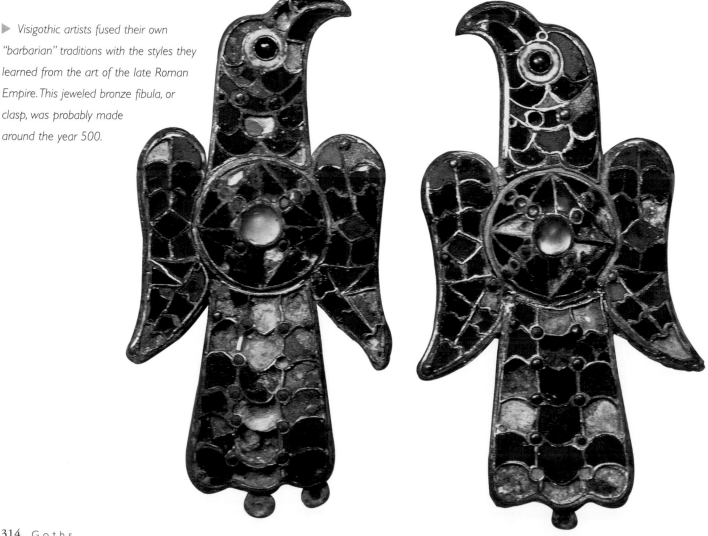

THE SACK OF ROME, 410 CE

The Visigoths under Alaric attacked Italy several times in the years 401 to 410. In 408 Alaric marched toward Rome, while the emperor Honorius and his court took refuge in the city of Ravenna in northern Italy. The city of Rome was without a leader and without an army to defend it.

The Roman citizens quickly strengthened the fortifications around their city, but Alaric cleverly captured the nearby port of Ostia. This move cut Rome off from ships bringing food and help. The city was besieged by the Goths while Alaric bargained with the emperor for riches and honors. By August 410 there was little food left inside the city, and there were rumors that some citizens had become cannibals.

On August 24 someone inside the city secretly opened the Salerian Gate, one of the twelve main entrances through the city wall. The Visigoths marched into the city, and three days of sack and plunder began. Palaces and temples were stripped of their gold and treasures, and many buildings were burned.

The Visigoth army badly needed fresh supplies of food and soon moved on toward the farmlands of Campania to the south. The world was shocked by news of the sack. Rome, for centuries one of the most powerful cities in the world, had been devastated by barbarians.

▼ This medieval fresco shows the central Italian city of Perugia under attack by Ostrogoths in the mid-6th century CE.

SEE ALSO
• Attila
• Constantine
• Huns
• Roman Republic and Empire

Great Wall of China

The Great Wall of China is the world's longest wall and largest human-made structure. The wall was built between the fifth century BCE and the seventeenth century CE. In ancient times it stretched fifteen hundred miles (2,400 km) from near the western city of Dunhuang eastward across northern China to the Yellow Sea.

The Great Wall was built on China's northern frontier to repel invasion by the nomadic tribes to the north. The idea was conceived by the first Chinese emperor, Cheng, also known as Qin Shi Huangdi, who ruled China from 221 to 210 BCE. Cheng did not start the wall from scratch. His plan was to build new sections to link existing walls that had been built since the fifth century BCE. Work on the Great Wall began around 214 BCE. In 207 Cheng's dynasty, the Qin, was overthrown by a new ruling family, the Han. Work on the wall continued under the Han, who ruled China from 206 BCE to 220 CE, and later under the Sui dynasty (589–618 CE) and the Ming (1368–1644 CE). Most of the Great Wall that visitors now see dates from the last period of its construction, under the Ming dynasty.

Structure of the Great Wall

The original Great Wall was built mostly of stone and earth and also brick, depending on the materials that were available locally. In the rocky, mountainous east the foundations were made of granite blocks. In the rolling deserts of the west, where stone was scarce, the wall was built mainly of compressed earth. Planners designed the wall to make use of natural features that formed a barrier, such as mountain ridges and deep gorges. In some areas a moat was dug on the outer, northern side. The finished wall towered up to thirty feet (9 m) high.

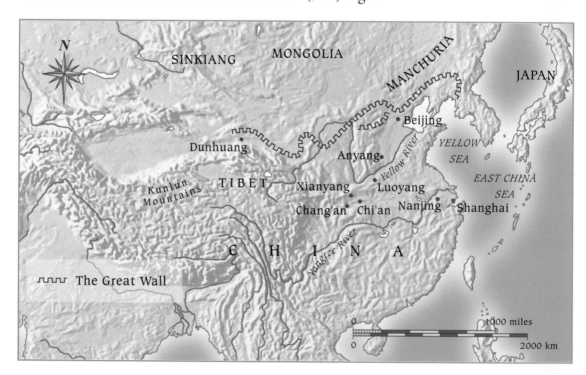

▶ This map shows the route of the Great Wall of China.

Tall watchtowers were built at intervals along the wall. These sentry positions were manned constantly. Soldiers who spotted an enemy approaching lit a fire that could be seen from the next watchtower, where sentries in turn lit their own beacon. As one beacon after another flared, warnings quickly passed along the length of the wall. At greater intervals, gateways were built to allow travelers to leave and enter China. The heavy wooden doors were closed and barred at night. A paved road protected by high walls ran along the top of the wall.

CONSTRUCTION DURING THE QIN DYNASTY

Under the Qin the building of the Great Wall was run like a military operation. Supply camps were set up to send food and supplies to the northern frontier where the wall was being built. Soldiers were posted to the wall to fight off raiding parties and to make sure that the thousands of peasants working on the wall did not escape.

Elephants and other pack animals helped to haul heavy timbers, which were used to make ramps and scaffolding. However, most of the thousands of tons of earth and stones used in construction were shifted by human muscle power alone.

家堅築圖

▲ *This painting shows workmen laboring on the Great Wall. The core of the wall was made of earth, which the workmen rammed into place by hand. They then hoisted up heavy stones to face the outside of the wall.*

The Building of the Wall

The construction of the Great Wall was an enormous undertaking. Hundreds of thousands of workers toiled over it for years, and many died during its construction. During Cheng's reign all adult men had to work on the wall and other public projects for a month each year. Only noblemen and civil servants did not have to help. Everyone also had to pay heavy taxes to finance the project. Raising the money caused great hardship among poor people. Soon after Cheng's death a peasant army rebelled against the Qin and overthrew Cheng's successor. The next dynasty, the Han, continued with the wall's construction but ruled with a lighter hand.

Uses of the Great Wall

The Great Wall did not prove very effective as a defensive barrier. It succeeded in keeping small raiding parties out, but large armies managed to break through many times during China's history. In the late fourth century CE nomadic tribes from the north broke through the wall, conquered northern China and held onto it for two centuries. China was divided into several smaller kingdoms until Sui emperors reunited it in 581 CE.

The raised road running along the top of the wall was much more successful, however. It provided a smooth, safe highway for soldiers, messengers, and other travelers journeying across northern China. Throughout ancient times the Great Wall formed a vital communications link between eastern and western regions of the vast Chinese empire.

SEE ALSO
• Cheng • China • Dunhuang

Glossary

adze A tool similar to an ax, with an arched blade set at right angles to the handle, used for trimming and shaping wood.

Apennines A mountain range that runs down the spine of Italy.

Archimedes' screw A device used to lift water from one level to another, consisting of a large continuous screw inside a cylinder. When the screw is turned, the water is lifted inside the cylinder by the spiral threads.

Arian A Christian who followed the outlawed teachings of Arius.

ashram An Indian word for a place where teaching is received.

chorus A group of performers, sometimes as many as fifty, who danced and commented in song, in groups or as one, on the action of a play

circus maximus A U-shaped amphitheater where chariot races were held.

duty work Every ancient Egyptian was expected to work for the pharaoh for a set number of days each year. This work could be building work, or work in the fields or clearing canals and ditches. Scribes were the only people who did not have to do duty work.

epic A long poem describing the adventures and deeds of a legendary hero or heroes.

fermentation The process of changing sugar into alcohol.

flax A plant with blue flowers that is widely cultivated for its seeds, which produce linseed oil, and its stems, from which fiber to make linen is obtained.

geometry The study of points, lines, angles, curves, surfaces, and solids in mathematics.

gymnasium From *gymnos*, meaning "naked," a Greek word meaning an area where young men exercised, had discussions, and heard lectures.

ibis A wading bird with a downward-curving bill.

Ionian A light, graceful building style using slender columns much admired and copied by the mainland Greeks and the Romans.

Italic Describing the people who lived in ancient Italy before and during Roman times.

map projection A representation of the curved surface of the earth on a flat, two-dimensional map. Ancient Greek geographers devised a number of different projections to show the world.

Ostrogoth A member of an eastern nomadic people from the Crimea region in southern Russia who moved into the Roman world after c. 150 CE.

pictograph A pictorial symbol used in writing to represent a group of words.

potsherd A fragment of pottery, especially one found at an archaeological site.

resin A sticky liquid that can be squeezed out of many plants and that hardens as it dries.

resurrection In Christian belief, the rising of Jesus from the dead after his crucifixion and entombment.

saffron An orange or yellow powder obtained from the saffron plant; used as a spice in cooking.

shadoof A water-raising device used in ancient Egypt consisting of a suspended pivoting pole with a bucket on one end and a counterweight on the other.

siege machine A movable wooden tower used to attack high city walls.

silted up Full of or obstructed with silt, a fine-grained sediment of mud or clay particles, deposited by running water.

Sivan The ninth month in the Jewish civic calendar. It falls within May and June

thresh Separate the seeds of a harvested plant from the straw and chaff, husks, or other residue.

Tishri The first month of the civic Jewish year, happening within September and October.

Visigoth A member of an eastern nomadic people related to the Ostrogoths. After entering the Roman world, the Visigoths eventually settled in Gaul and the Iberian peninsula.

Vulcan In Roman mythology, the god of fire.

Index

Page numbers in **boldface type** refer to main articles.
Page numbers in *italic type* refer to illustrations.